THE 250 QUESTIONS

EVERYONE SHOULD ASK ABOUT

BUYING FORECLOSURES

Lita Epstein, M.B.A.

BUSINESS

Avon, Massachusetts

2/09 ᴌᴀᴅ — — ͦ˙ᴰ
9/10 ℓᴀᴅ ²/₁₀ . 4 ②

Published by Adams Business
An imprint of Adams Media, an F+W Publications Company
57 Littlefield Street, Avon, MA 02322. U.S.A.
www.adamsmedia.com

ISBN 10: 1-59869-583-5
ISBN 13: 978-1-59869-583-0

Printed in the United States of America.

J   I   H   G   F   E   D   C   B   A

Library of Congress Cataloging-in-Publication Data
is available from the publisher.

This book is available at quantity discounts for bulk purchases.
For information, call 1–800–289–0963.

CONTENTS

INTRODUCTION

As the number of foreclosures on the market continued to grow through 2007 with expectations for even more in 2008, the market for buying a foreclosure could never be better. While many banks were forced to buy the property at auction because the mortgage was actually higher than the home value, the bargains after the auction sale make for some interesting buys. Pre-foreclosure short sales were also on the rise in 2007, as banks preferred to take less than the amount due and avoid the foreclosure process completely.

This book will help you sort through the different ways you can buy a pre-foreclosure and post-foreclosure property. You'll also learn the basic terminologies unique to the foreclosure market to help you understand what you're seeing throughout the purchase and contract process.

Yes you can make money buying foreclosures even in a real estate downturn, but you must be ready to do some minor repairs yourself or have a good group of contractors that can help you. You also should be prepared to hold the property and rent it for a while until the buyers' market for real estate turns back to a sellers' market and prices again start to rise.

Good luck and happy foreclosure hunting!

Chapter 1

REVIEWING MORTGAGE BASICS

You've probably bought a home several times throughout your lifetime, and you probably hate sitting through the closing and signing your life away on pages and pages of documents filled with legalese you've probably never read in their entirety. But if you plan to start buying foreclosures, it's time to pay more attention to the details in those mortgage contracts.

This chapter covers the basics of the documents that are signed at closing, how they affect one's ownership rights, and what happens to those rights when someone doesn't pay. When you buy a foreclosure, you are actually taking advantage of someone else's loss because of what's in those documents.

Question 1. What is a mortgage?

You may not realize this, but a mortgage is a type of loan. In this situation, the loan is used to purchase property, and the property being purchased is used as a guarantee for the loan amount. This guarantee then becomes a lien against the property.

After all the papers are signed at closing, the lien gets recorded in public records, most likely at the county courthouse where the property is located. The buyer can't sell that home to anyone else until that debt is paid in full and the lien is released.

The person who has the mortgage does have full title to the property, but the mortgage contract does give the lender the right to sell the secured property to recover funds if payments are not made on the debt. When you buy a foreclosure, it means that someone did not pay their debt; by selling the home to you, the lender is recovering the funds lost on the original mortgage. When you buy the foreclosure, you will likely take another mortgage to pay for that home.

There are numerous types of mortgages on the market, including fixed-rate mortgages, balloon mortgages, adjustable-rate mortgages, and interest-only mortgages:

- Fixed-rate mortgages are mortgages in which the interest rate is set when the loan is taken and remains the same throughout the life of the loan. This is usually fifteen, twenty, or thirty years, but other lengths can be worked out with the financial institution.
- Balloon mortgages are mortgages in which an interest rate is set for a specific period of time. At the end of that period, the total amount of the mortgage is due.
- Adjustable-rate mortgages, also known as ARMs, are mortgages in which the interest rate changes periodically. Most commonly, ARMs are set to adjust rates either annually; or once after three years, and annually thereafter; or once after five years and annually thereafter. With this type of loan, the interest rate is pegged to some standard rate, such as a certain percentage above the prime rate.
- Interest-only mortgages are mortgages in which only the interest portion of the loan is paid and none of the principal amount due on the mortgage. The danger with this type of mortgage is that if the value of a house falls below

what you paid for it, the person who is buying the home may need to come up with cash to sell their home.

Question 2. **What is a deed of trust?**

In about half the states, a deed of trust is used instead of a mortgage. As with a mortgage, the deed of trust is recorded in public records to tell everyone that there is a lien on a piece of property.

The deed of trust actually involves three parties. The person buying the home who takes out the loan is the trustor; the financial institution that provides the money for the loan is called the beneficiary; and a neutral third party is the trustee. The trustee is someone who temporarily holds title (but not full title) until the lien is paid.

The deed of trust is cancelled when the person buying the house finishes paying the loan. Until that time, the trustee holds the power to foreclose on the debt if the trustor doesn't make the payments. When a deed of trust is used rather than a mortgage, the trustee can foreclose on the loan without having to go to court, so it makes it easier and faster to foreclose on a home secured by a deed of trust than by a mortgage.

Question 3. **What is a grant deed?**

The grant deed is the document that actually transfers the ownership title to a real estate property from one party, who is known as the grantor, to another party, who is known as the grantee.

The grant deed must describe the property by legal description of boundaries and/or parcel numbers. All people who are involved in the transfer of the property must sign the grant deed, which must be acknowledged before a notary public.

The transfer of ownership of the property is completed when the grant deed is recorded with the county recorder or recorder of deeds. The grant deed warrants that the grantor actually owned the title to the property and that it is not encumbered in any way unless stated in the grant deed.

In some situations, when you buy a home, you will see something called a quitclaim deed. In this type of deed, the ownership interest a person has in a particular property is transferred, but there is no guarantee of what is being transferred. Most commonly, the quitclaim deed in seen in a situation in which a divorcing spouse quitclaims his or her interest in a particular piece of property to his or her ex-spouse, which means he or she has given up a legal interest in that property.

Question 4. **What is a warranty deed?**

The warranty deed is the most common type of deed you will see when dealing with residential real estate. In this type of deed, the grantor (seller) guarantees that he or she holds clear title to the real estate property being sold and has a right to sell it to you. The guarantee is not limited to the time the grantor owned the property. The guarantee extends back in time to the property's origins of ownership.

When you do get a warranty deed, it should include these statements:

- There are no hidden liens or encumbrances on the property, which means you should not find out about any debts or other holds on the property other than those that you see in public records. For example, the seller guarantees that a distant cousin won't show up years later and claim that she still owns part of the property.
- The grantor declares he or she owns the property and has the right to sell it to you.
- The grantor guarantees that if the title ever fails, he or she will compensate you as the grantee (new property owner) for any losses incurred defending your title to the property. (If there are title problems in the future, this guarantee

might not mean much if the grantor is dead or unable to follow through with his or her promise.)

Question 5. **What is a loan broker?**

A loan broker is a financial professional who does not work for one particular lender but who instead seeks to find you the best rate for the type of mortgage you want from numerous potential lenders. A good loan broker will help you sort through the pros and cons of various loan products available and help you determine which product best meets your needs and individual circumstances. When you work with a loan broker, you will have the greatest number of options and terms available.

After you determine what type of loan you want, the loan broker will then make contact for you with a number of potential lenders who offer that product. He or she will then help you determine which of the financial alternatives is best for you.

The big difference when you work with an individual loan broker, as opposed to a lending institution like a bank, is that the broker is not tied to one particular lender (like a particular bank) and can thus be more creative in finding you the best deal.

Question 6. **What is a lender?**

Any institution or individual who loans you money can be considered a lender. The most common type of lender in the mortgage business is a commercial lender, which is usually a banking institution but can sometimes be a private financial group. When you use this type of lender, you will get an offer for a loan with certain terms that include the interest rate you will be charged and the length of the loan.

If you are considering a balloon loan, you may end up dealing with a hard-money lender, who specializes in short-term loans that are backed primarily with real estate as collateral. Be careful, though. A hard-money lender generally offers worse rates than a traditional bank institution; at the same time, this kind of lender also tends to offer more flexible terms and is more willing to back riskier loan situations, such as someone with a bad credit history.

If you belong to a community credit union, you may find lower loan rates than you can through a commercial bank. These mutual organizations are nonprofit and able to give higher rates on savings and lower rates on loans.

Another source for people with very low credit scores is a lender of last resort. These are private institutions that loan to people who are considered to be in extremely high risk of default. Your loan terms for this type of loan will include exorbitant interest rates.

Question 7. **What is a servicing lender?**

The servicing lender is the one responsible for collecting all your payments and for being sure those payments are properly applied. Servicing lenders also make sure that borrowers are in compliance with the stipulations in the loan agreements.

If there is a problem with a loan, such as a potential foreclosure or bankruptcy, the servicing lender is the one that makes sure the interests of the investor (lender) are protected. When you are negotiating terms for buying a foreclosure, you will have to negotiate with the servicing lender and satisfy its demands, as well as those of the lender whose investment is at stake.

Question 8. **What is a promissory note?**

A promissory note is often used in conjunction with a mortgage. Basically, a promissory note used when buying a home is a contract that details the terms of the repayment of the property loan. The note includes the principal amount, the interest rate, and the maturity date (the date the loan must be paid in full). The party who promises to pay is called the maker, and the party he or she will be paying is called the payee.

In addition to the loan terms, you will likely see provisions concerning the rights of the payee to collect his or her money in the case of a default, which usually includes the foreclosure of the maker's interest in the property. The difference between a promissory note and an IOU is that the IOU is just an acknowledgement of the existence of a debt that you owe, while a promissory note includes a promise that you will pay the amount stated.

When a promissory note is used in conjunction with a mortgage, it is written as a negotiable instrument governed by Article 3 of the Uniform Commercial Code. A negotiable promissory note can be sold to a third party, who then has the rights of the payee to collect on the debt.

Question 9. **What is an institutional lender?**

Any institution that lends money for an interest fee and whose loans are regulated by law, such as a commercial bank, savings bank, a life insurance company, or a savings-and-loan association, is an institutional lender. Pension and trust funds can also fit under the umbrella as an institutional lender.

To qualify as an institutional lender, an organization must lend money received from its depositors. This is the difference that distinguishes institutional lenders from private lenders who lend their own money.

Question 10. **What is a private lender?**

A private lender is someone who lends you the money to buy your real estate, with the money loaned coming from the lender's private funds. Your rates will be higher, but your terms for the loan may be better given your financial situation. If you are buying foreclosure properties for investment purposes, a private lender may be the only one who will loan you money for this riskier purpose. For example, the private lender may be more willing to make the loan even if you are putting no money down or your credit history is not perfect.

The biggest advantage of private lending is the minimal approval process and the speed with which you can get an answer. You also don't have to pay a loan origination fee, or points.

There is no limit to the number of mortgages you can get from private lenders, as mortgages through private lenders don't show up on your credit report. But you should expect to pay a higher interest rate for a mortgage from a private lender than you would for one from an institutional lender.

Question 11. **What is a conventional loan?**

Loans that are secured by government-sponsored entities (GSEs), such as Fannie Mae or Freddie Mac, are called conventional loans. These types of loans can be used to purchase or refinance single-family homes and multifamily homes up to homes for four families.

Each year Fannie Mae and Freddie Mac set a limit for a mortgage loan, which in 2007 was $417,000 for a single-family home. The limit is reviewed annually and changed, if necessary, to reflect the average price of single-family homes. Conventional loan limits in 2007 for first mortgages on homes larger than single family were as follows: $533,850 for two-family homes; $645,300 for three-family homes; and $801,950 for four-family homes. If the home loan was for property in Alaska, Hawaii, Guam, and the U.S. Virgin Islands, then the original loan amount could be 50 percent higher for the first mortgage.

Conventional loans for second mortgages are also available through GSEs. The maximum conventional loan for a second mortgage was $208,500 in 2007, but if the home was in Alaska, Hawaii, or the U.S. Virgin Islands, the maximum was $312,750.

If you are looking for a loan higher than these amounts, you can get a jumbo loan. These loans are not funded by the GSEs and usually carry higher interest rates, as well as additional underwriting requirements, which means you've got to jump through more hoops to qualify for the loan.

Question 12. **What is an FHA loan?**

Buyers can buy a house with less money down if they buy a home using a U.S. Federal Housing Administration (FHA) loan. These government loans are geared primarily to first-time homebuyers or to buyers who don't have enough money to put down on a home and qualify for a conventional loan. The FHA allows buyers to put down as little as 3 percent. Otherwise, a buyer puts 5 percent down for a conventional loan.

In actuality, the FHA does not make home loans. Instead, it insures the loans that a bank makes. If a person defaults on his or her payments, the lending institution then gets paid from an insurance fund established by the FHA.

If you plan to buy a foreclosure that was originally an FHA loan, you will have different hoops to jump through than with a foreclosure that was originally a conventional loan. The unique aspects of buying an FHA foreclosure are discussed in greater detail in questions 37, 38, and 113.

Question 13. **What is a VA loan?**

A VA loan is a loan program for veterans that gives veterans a way to buy homes without providing a down payment, as long as the purchase price is more than the reasonable value of the property, which is determined by the U.S. Department of Veterans Affairs (VA). These loans are fixed-interest rate loans that are competitive with conventional mortgage rates.

Most VA loans are assumable, but the person buying the home who wants to assume a VA loan must prove his or her creditworthiness, which means that the buyer must be able and willing to make the payments on the loan. If you are a veteran who permits your VA loan to be assumed, you cannot apply for another VA loan until the first loan is paid off.

If someone holds a VA loan and is experiencing temporary financial difficulty, the VA will usually be more lenient toward the homeowner than will a commercial or private lender. You can find out more about VA loans at the VA Web site (*www.homeloans. va.gov*). So if you are considering buying a foreclosure of a property financed through the VA, expect it to take longer and expect to jump through more hoops. If you are successful, however, you may be able to assume the VA mortgage. The specifics of buying a VA foreclosure are discussed in greater detail in questions 37, 114, and 142.

Question 14. **What is the difference between a first, second, and third mortgage or loan?**

When a person initially buys a home, the mortgage or loan that is arranged is called the *first* or *senior mortgage*. The mortgage holder is this case has first rights to any money from the sale of the property, whether the property is sold or the debt is foreclosed on for nonpayment of the debt.

Any money borrowed in addition to the first money becomes *junior debt*. The first loan after the first mortgage is called a *second mortgage*. This is commonly the case with an equity line of credit. In this case, the lender is subordinate to the first mortgage lender, which means when the property is sold or the property is foreclosed on, the second mortgage lender will only get paid with funds left after the first mortgage lender is paid off.

If a third loan is taken, it becomes subordinate to both the first and second mortgage. In this case, the lender on the third mortgage or loan will only get paid after the first and second mortgage lenders are paid. If you are considering buying a foreclosure, be certain you are aware of all the loans on a property. Even if an arrangement is made with the first mortgage lender, if the second or third mortgage lender does not sign off on the agreement, you could be stuck with that debt.

Question 15. **What is private mortgage insurance?**

Anytime someone purchases a home with less than a 20 percent down payment, a lender will probably require that the buyer get private mortgage insurance (PMI). This insurance is not paid to the person who defaults on his payments. It is paid to the lending institution that originally made the loan. If PMI insurance is involved, that could complicate the foreclosure agreement. Question 97 covers this subject more extensively.

Question 16. **What is an assumable loan?**

A mortgage that allows you to take over the obligation of the existing loan without a change in loan terms is an assumable loan. These are loans that do not have a due-on-sale clause, which means the loan must be paid off in order for the property to be sold. Assumable loans are an excellent opportunity if you are planning to buy a foreclosure property that is financed with a loan with a fixed interest rate below those currently available on the market.

Few loans today are assumable. You are most likely to find assumable loans if you are considering buying a property financed using an FHA or VA mortgage.

Question 17. **What is a prepayment penalty?**

Some mortgage loans require you to a pay a penalty if you pay them off early. This is called a prepayment penalty. Most often you will find these penalties on loans in which the borrower secured the loan with very low closing costs. The prepayment penalty is required if the loan is paid off in a very short time period, such as three to five years.

If the foreclosure you are considering has a prepayment penalty, you will find the provision spelled out in the loan documents, as well as in the truth-in-lending statement. Many people don't save all their paperwork at closing, or they can't find it for you to inspect prior to purchasing the property. You definitely need to find out whether a loan carries a prepayment penalty because it could mean a significant cash payment at closing you were not anticipating. Check with the lender of any property you are considering to be sure there is no prepayment penalty.

Chapter **2**

UNDERSTANDING FORECLOSURE BASICS

When buying a foreclosure, you are a player in the game of life, where someone will lose his or her home. While you might be excited about the investment potential if you can get the home cheaply, always remember that you are dealing with a family or individual facing financial hardship. This chapter covers the basics of foreclosure, how it works, and what you can expect if you plan to buy a home nearing foreclosure.

Question 18. **What is foreclosure?**

Foreclosure is the means by which a lender can legally repossess (take ownership) of a home if the borrower isn't living up to his end of the bargain—making payments to the bank on time. Once the bank forecloses on a home, the borrower can be evicted from the home. The eviction process differs from state to state. Details are discussed further on a state-by-state basis in Chapter 12.

There are two possible types of foreclosures. One type is called *deed in lieu of foreclosure*, or *judicial foreclosure*. The second is called a *nonjudicial foreclosure*. These two procedures are discussed in greater detail throughout this chapter. In either case, the property will likely be auctioned to the highest bidder by the county sheriff or some other officer of the court. Often the bank or other lending institution bids on the house at the auction at the price of the debt owed. If no other buyer bids higher, the bank wins the property.

Question 19. **What is pre-foreclosure?**

Pre-foreclosure is the period between the time when the lender notifies the borrower that it filed a foreclosure lawsuit or a notice of default in the official public records and the time when the property is to be sold at auction. The notice of default includes the actual date the property will be sold at a public foreclosure auction or trustee's sale.

A borrower may still be able to stop a foreclosure after getting the notice of default. That's when you, as a potential investor who wants to buy the property, have the best opportunity to make an offer on a property. Borrowers can sell the property themselves or can consider filing for bankruptcy to stop the foreclosure process. (Bankruptcy is discussed in greater detail in Chapter 9.)

Question 20. **What are the four phases of foreclosure?**

You can buy a foreclosure property in each of the four phases of foreclosure: pre-foreclosure, default stage, auction or trustee's sale, and as real estate owner (REO) property (discussed in question 139). The best time to try to work out a deal with an owner, when you can inspect the property thoroughly before purchase, is in the pre-foreclosure period. During this time, the mortgage is delinquent, but the official foreclosure process has not yet started. The process of buying a pre-foreclosure is discussed in greater detail in Chapter 5.

Once the legal foreclosure process has begun, things have entered the default stage. You may still be able to work out a deal with the owner, but you will also have to work with the lender's loan mitigation to complete a purchase. This is the time when you might have the best chance of working out a short-payoff. This is because the lender usually prefers to avoid the auction process and the legal costs involved, as well as the uncertainty of what it can get for the property and whether the property will sell at all. The short-payoff option is discussed in greater detail in Chapter 6.

The third phase is the formal sale of a foreclosure—the auction or trustee's sale. If you wait for that phase, you have no control over the price or over how many others will try to bid on the property. The highest bid will win the property, so if you think you've found a good buy, it's best to work out a deal before the auction. The auction process is discussed in greater detail in Chapter 7.

You can sometimes get some great bargains if the bank ends up buying the property at the auction and then needs to sell it. This is called real estate owned (REO) property. Chapter 8 discusses the procedures for buying property in that phase.

Question 21. **How do most lenders handle delinquent loans?**

When a mortgage payment is between thirty-five and forty-five days late, the borrower gets a borrower information packet from the bank that indicates the status of his mortgage. In addition, the borrower gets information on how to "cure" the default, which lists options for getting the loan back on track.

If you are discussing buying a home before foreclosure with the owner, use the information in the packet to find the necessary contact numbers for the lender's loss-mitigation department. That's the department you'll have to work with to determine terms for taking over the loan or buying the home and refinancing.

Question 22. **What are demand letters?**

Borrowers nearing foreclosure will get a letter that states the entire balance of their loan and states the fact it is due and payable immediately. This is called a *demand letter,* or, sometimes, a *notice of acceleration* because it is based on the acceleration clause of a mortgage contract. This clause describes the situations under which the borrower is considered in default. If the clause does exist in a mortgage, it allows the lender to accelerate, or push forward, the date that a mortgage must be paid in full.

If you find out about a family in trouble and decide their home is a good investment for you, you can buy that home in this pre-foreclosure situation. Find out if the family has gotten a demand letter. That letter will give you a lot of the financial details you will need to determine what financial obligations you will be required to meet before buying the property.

Question 23. **What is default status?**

Once mortgage payments are ninety days late, a mortgage loan is considered in default status, and the foreclosure process can begin. At this point, the loan is in delinquent status.

Most lenders transfer the servicing of a loan in delinquent status from the regular servicer to a special servicer. The borrower will get a letter in the mail giving them contact information for the loss-mitigation department.

The special servicer is the one that decides on the final disposition of the loan and whether or not to start the foreclosure process. You can work with this special servicer to negotiate terms for buying the property prior to foreclosure.

Question 24. **Can a loan be reinstated that is in default status?**

From the time a borrower receives the notice that his or her mortgage is in default to five days prior to the foreclosure sale, the borrower *can* reinstate the loan. The simplest way to reinstate a mortgage loan is to pay all past-due payments and penalties in full. A person can find out exactly how much is due to reinstate the loan by talking with the special servicer. As the person who wants to buy the foreclosure, this information will give you the ammunition you need to negotiate to buy the property.

Question 25. **What is a notice of default?**

A notice of default, which for most conventional loans is sent when a borrower is ninety to ninety-five days past due on his or her last loan payment, sets the process of foreclosure in motion. Once a lender notifies someone that he is in default, the lender also tells its attorney or trustee to initiate the foreclosure process. The notice of default is used in a nonjudicial foreclosure action. (See question 32.)

The notice of default will likely start like so: "If your property is in foreclosure because you are behind in your payments, it may be sold without any court action, and you have the legal right to bring your account in good standing by paying all of your past-due payments plus permitted costs and expenses within the time permitted by law for reinstatement of your account." Normally, the borrower is given three months before an actual sale takes place and has up to five days before the sale to reinstate his or her account.

The notice of default also states the amount due as of a specific date and specifies that the amount will increase until the account becomes current. The borrower is instructed how to get a statement of the full amount due at any time during the three-month period prior to the sale of the property that he is in default. He will also find instructions on how to stop the sale of the property by paying the full amount due.

Question 26. **How does a notice of default work?**

After the borrower receives the notice of default, the lender's attorney then files the notice of default in the county in which the property is located. This becomes public record for all to see. This gives the public constructive notice that a mortgage or deed is in default. The notice also includes a schedule of when the property will be foreclosed, which in most cases will be through a private trustee's auction.

The notice of default is then sent by certified or registered mail, postage prepaid and return receipt requested, to the current owner, mortgagors of record, and all dwelling units that are secured by the mortgage in default. All other lien holders are also sent information about the foreclosure sale.

Question 27. **What information is included in a foreclosure notice?**

A foreclosure notice contains detailed information about the borrower, the property, and the loan involved in the foreclosure. This information includes the following details:

- Date the notice of default or lawsuit (lis pendens) was filed and recorded in the public records
- Names and addresses of the mortgagor or trustor whose loan is in default
- Names and address of the lender, trustee, or beneficiary that is foreclosing on the loan
- Notice of default or case number
- Street address of the property
- Legal description of the property
- Land use or zoning code for the property
- Value of the property in the tax assessor's records
- Original amount of the loan
- Date the original loan was made
- Date the last payment was made on the loan
- Amount of past-due payments
- Balance of the loan at the time the foreclosure action is filed
- Date of the public foreclosure auction or trustee's sale

Question 28. **Are foreclosure notices published in the newspaper?**

In most states, the notice of default and information about the foreclosure sale are published once a week for three successive calendar weeks before the date of the foreclosure sale. This publication requirement can vary from state to state. The publication chosen for this notice must have general circulation in the county or counties in which the property in question is located.

The newspaper chosen should be conducive to providing notice of foreclosure to interested parties. For example, a newspaper that is generally accepted as the newspaper of legal record for the county or counties in which the property to be sold is located would be considered an appropriate newspaper. If you are interested in buying foreclosures in a particular county and are not sure where the notice of defaults are published, check with staff in the county clerk's office. If there is no newspaper appropriate for this circulation, then a notice of default or foreclosure will be posted at the courthouse of the county or counties in which the property is located and at the place where the property sale will be held.

Question 29. **What is a mortgage estoppel letter?**

A mortgage estoppel letter from the trustor or lender verifies the type of loan, any unpaid principal loan balance, interest rate, principal and interest payment, insurance payment, tax payment, payment due date, escrow impound balance, and total monthly payment. This letter also includes the amount of loan payment past due, the total amount of accrued interest, late charges, penalties, and legal fees owed.

When negotiating with a property owner to buy a home prior to foreclosure, you should always ask for a copy of this letter so you know exactly what needs to be paid off. This letter guarantees that you are getting full information about the outstanding loan so you don't face any surprises at closing. If the homeowner does not have a copy of this letter, ask him or her to request it from the lender's loan mitigation department.

Question 30. **What must a lender do before foreclosing on or repossessing a home?**

The first step a lender takes toward foreclosing on a property is to send a notice of default (for a nonjudicial foreclosure) or file a lawsuit (for a judicial foreclosure). The process for both types of foreclosures is discussed throughout this chapter.

Once documentation of one of these steps is filed with the county in which the property is located, the foreclosure begins. If the property is located in a state that allows nonjudicial foreclosure, then the borrower enters the reinstatement period, which is a period of about three months before the home is sold by the trustee or lender at auction.

At the end of the three-month period, if the borrower does not cure the loan (that is, get the loan up to date or work out a payment plan with the lender), a *notice of trustee sale* is sent, which gives the date, time, and location of the sale of the property.

For full details on the nonjudicial foreclosure process, see question 34. If you are considering purchasing foreclosure property in a state that requires a judicial foreclosure process, see question 32 for more details on how that process works.

Question 31. **What is judicial foreclosure?**

Lenders must use the judicial foreclosure process if the state in which the property is located requires the use of judicial foreclosure. Chapter 12 reviews the foreclosure rules of each state. Twenty-four states require judicial foreclosures, and five states have provisions for both judicial and nonjudicial foreclosures depending upon the mortgage or trust documents.

A judicial foreclosure requires a court action to repossess a person's property. These types of foreclosures are required when a trust deed or mortgage does not have a power-of-sale clause, which means the lender must take the borrower to court. This can be a much more lengthy and costly process than a nonjudicial foreclosure.

The judicial foreclosure process starts when a lender files a lawsuit to foreclose and names the borrower in default, which could be a mortgagor or trustor, as the defendant. Other defendants could be any lien holders of record that have an interest in the property.

Question 32. **How does the judicial foreclosure process work?**

Once the lender files a lawsuit, the borrower and any other defendants usually have twenty days to reply formally to the lawsuit and present their case. If there is no reply to the suit, the judge rules against the defendant and orders that the mortgage or deed of trust be foreclosed on. The property is then sold at auction.

The borrower's attorney will reply to the lawsuit on his behalf, and a court hearing date will be set. The timing of this hearing varies from state to state, depending on the backlog of cases. Once the case is heard in court, the judge will either order that the loan be foreclosed on or dismiss the case.

If the judge rules against the borrower and orders the loan to be foreclosed on, the public-foreclosure auction sale will be scheduled by the county sheriff or another party designated for that purpose by the county in which the property is located.

Public foreclosure auction sales are advertised, and the property is sold to the highest bidder at the auction. Alternately, if there are no acceptable bids from auction participants, it may be taken back by the lender. The judge may also award the lender a deficiency judgment against the borrower if the bid that is accepted is less than the amount owed.

After the sale, some states give borrowers statutory redemption rights. To exercise these rights, the borrower must pay off the entire unpaid balance of the loan plus late fees, penalties, attorney fees, and trustee costs. While borrowers don't have the legal right to reinstate their loan during the redemption period, some lenders may permit them to do so.

If there is a statutory redemption period, the sheriff's deed or certificate of title is given to the highest bidder as soon as that period expires. If there is no statutory redemption period, then the highest bidder will get the deed or title immediately after the sale. It's important that you find out whether or not your state allows redemptions. If so, be aware that you could lose the property even if you win the auction in the case that a borrower is able to find the money needed to redeem the loan.

Question 33. **What is nonjudicial foreclosure?**

A nonjudicial foreclosure permits the lender or trustee to foreclose on a property without having to go to court by invoking the power-of-sale clause in the mortgage or deed of trust. Twenty-two states and the District of Columbia (Washington, D.C.) permit a nonjudicial foreclosure. (See Chapter 12 for the rules in your state.) Five states allow both judicial and nonjudicial foreclosures, depending upon the mortgage or deed of trust documents. If a nonjudicial foreclosure is permitted, the borrower will find a power-of-sale clause in his mortgage or trust documents.

Question 34. **How does the nonjudicial foreclosure process work?**

A nonjudicial foreclosure starts after the notice of default is sent to the borrower, mortgagor, or trustor, and is then filed with the county or counties in which the property is located. After the notice of default is filed, the borrower then has about three months to reinstate the loan. The actual time allowed for reinstatement and public trustee sale varies state by state, but three months is the most common time period. (See Chapter 12 for details about your state.)

About twenty to twenty-five days before the end of the reinstatement period, a public trustee's sale date is set and a notice of trustee sale is recorded with the county or counties in which the property is located. The notice of trustee sale is also sent to the borrower. The public trustee's sale is then advertised.

The property is then sold to the highest bidder at the public trustee's sale or taken back by the lender if there are no acceptable bids from the public. If there are statutory redemption rights after the sale, the buyer will then be given time to redeem based on these rights. To redeem the property, the buyer must pay off the entire balance of his loan, plus all late fees, penalties, attorney fees, and trustee's costs.

Question 35. **What is a power-of-sale foreclosure?**

A power-of-sale foreclosure is one in which a *power-of-sale* clause does exist in the mortgage or deed of trust. This clause specifies exactly what steps are needed in order to foreclose on the property.

When a power-of-sale clause does exist, the procedures for a nonjudicial foreclosure are followed, as discussed in question 34. For a nonjudicial disclosure to go forward, the loan default must be proven, and the borrower must be notified using a notice of default.

Question 36. **What is a no-power-of-sale foreclosure?**

If there is no power-of-sale clause in the mortgage or deed of trust, then a no-power-of-sale foreclosure must be started. If the property is in a state where judicial foreclosures are required, then the process of a no-power-of-sale foreclosure must follow the steps discussed in question 32.

If the property is located in a nonjudicial state or in a state in which the lender has the option to foreclose using the procedures of a nonjudicial or judicial foreclosure, the lender must decide which process he will use and must then follow the rules for that process. In most cases, given a choice, the lender will choose the nonjudicial foreclosure process, which costs less, is simpler, and usually takes less time. But if there are multiple owners of the property, or multiple lien holders, the lender may prefer to use a judicial foreclosure process to sort out all the issues involved.

Question 37. How do FHA and VA foreclosure rules differ from conventional loans?

Both FHA (U.S. Federal Housing Administration) and VA (U.S. Department of Veterans Affairs) home mortgages are backed by the government, which means the government will reimburse the bank for 100 percent of the loan if a borrower defaults on the mortgage.

In the case of FHA loans, these reimbursements come out of a fund that is funded by insurance premiums collected at a mortgage's original closing. Borrowers must pay the insurance premium at closing (which is usually financed as part of the mortgage), and insurance premiums are then paid into a fund that is used to pay off lenders if a borrower defaults. In the case of VA loans, the loan guarantee is a benefit offered all veterans for which they do not need to pay any premiums.

For both types of loans, the borrower will have access to extensive counseling to try to keep his home and avoid foreclosure. FHA lenders must follow an extensive set of procedures before foreclosing on a property, including special forbearance agreements and mortgage modifications, and the process provides many opportunities to avoid foreclosures as long as the borrower cooperates with the lending institution and works with a housing counseling agency. VA Regional Loan Centers assist veterans who are experiencing financial difficulties to help them avoid foreclosure.

Question 38. How does the FHA counsel borrowers on the verge of defaulting?

You don't have to wait until you are facing foreclosure to seek help from a HUD (U.S. Department of Housing and Urban Development) housing counseling agency. Agencies are located in every state and can provide you with assistance on defaults and credit issues, as well as foreclosures.

Borrowers can get help on alternatives such as home-equity conversion mortgage counseling, loss-mitigation, relocation counseling, money and debt management, mortgage delinquency and default resolution counseling, and predatory lending mitigation. Some counseling agencies are also charity organizations and may be able to help the borrower with financial assistance to get through a bad period.

You can find out more about HUD counseling agencies near you by going online to *www.hud.gov/offices/hsg/sfh/hcc/hcs.cfm*. Your local phone book should also list the number of the HUD office nearest you.

Question 39. **What is special forbearance?**

If an FHA borrower loses his job or experiences another type of temporary loss of income or unexpected financial expense, such as a health emergency, he may be able to request a special forbearance agreement from his lender. The agreement may reduce or delay the borrower's monthly payments for a specified period of time. This process is called a special forbearance. In order for a special forbearance to be requested, the borrower must have at least three payments due and unpaid.

In most cases, this agreement requires that the borrower repay any missed payments over a set number of months. These repayments will be added to the regular monthly payments as part of a repayment plan.

A special forbearance fails if the mortgagor abandons the property, the mortgagor advises the mortgagee that he will not follow through and fulfill the term's agreement, or the mortgagor allows an installment that is part of the agreement to become due and unpaid for sixty consecutive days from the payment date. After that sixty-day period, the mortgagee has ninety days to initiate a foreclosure.

If you are working with a homeowner who decides to try to save his home, he may decide to attempt to negotiate a special forbearance agreement. Stay in touch with the homeowner through this process because if he fails to get such an agreement, you will find it an excellent time to work out an agreement to purchase the home.

Question 40. **What is a due-on-sale or acceleration clause?**

The due-on-sale or acceleration clause is a provision in a loan agreement or promissory note that specifies that when a certain event happens, such as a borrower's failure to make payments on time, the lender has the right to require that the entire amount due must be paid immediately. This is a common clause in documents used for the purchase of real estate property.

The due-on-sale or acceleration clause can require that the property be sold in order to pay the note immediately. Some states prohibit the due-on-sale clause and instead allow a new property owner to assume the debt. You can find out more about your state's rules in Chapter 12.

Chapter **3**

LOOKING AT LIENS

You can be faced with a lien on your own property, or you may find that a property you plan to buy has one or more liens against it. You must understand how those liens came about and what you can do to clear the title to that property. If you are buying foreclosure properties, don't be surprised to find numerous liens that must be cleared before you can close on the property. This chapter explains the various types of liens and how you can end up with one against a property you own or intend to buy.

Question 41. **What are statutory liens?**

Statutory liens are those that creditors can get to obtain a security interest in your assets to satisfy a debt based on state and, sometimes, federal laws. The two most commonly used statutory liens are mechanic's liens and tax liens. If you try to buy property on which a statutory lien has been placed, the lien holder will have to be paid off at the closing. You must consider that payoff when determining how much you offer on the property and how much the homeowner will get out of the property. If the homeowner is taking a loss on the property, you will probably have to come up with the cash to cover the lien in order to close on the property.

A statutory lien will be considered invalid if it has not been filed with the appropriate government office, a process also known as *perfected*. Mechanic's liens usually must be filed within sixty to ninety days after the work is performed and acted on within one year. See question 48 about the process for mechanic's liens. Tax liens can be filed up to two to three years after they are due. If not paid, the government agency can foreclose on the property and sell it for the value of the taxes.

Question 42. **What are equitable liens?**

An equitable lien against a property means a debt is owed, but the homeowner maintains possession of the property. The debtor cannot foreclose on the property to collect on the lien.

An equitable lien can be express or implied. An express equitable lien is one based on a written contract. For example, suppose you buy a large-screen television with a personal check and state (express) on the contract of sale that if the check is no good, the store owner will have a lien against your home. This type of lien is recognized as a secure transaction.

An implied equitable lien is one that must be declared by a court and is based on the conduct and dealings of the parties. Whether an express or implied equitable lien, the property in question remains in the possession of the debtor, but the property owner cannot remove or change the property in question without the permission of the debtor. If you find an equitable lien on a property you are considering buying, you will need to be certain that the lien is satisfied before purchasing the property.

Question 43. **What are specific liens?**

A specific lien is any lien that is placed against a certain property. Many different types of liens are specific liens, including a mechanic's lien, trust deed, attachment, property tax lien, and lis pendens. This differs from a general lien, which affects all property of an owner, such as a judgment lien or federal or state income tax liens.

Question 44. **What are general liens?**

A general lien comes from everyday transactions that you engage in as part of your general course of business rather than relate to a specific transaction or property. In business, professionals who do work for you, such as attorneys, accountants, or bankers, are most likely to use a general lien.

For example, when an attorney or accountant wants to be certain to be paid for his work, the professional can retain possession of papers and personal property that you have given him in order for him to perform those professional services until payment is received. This would be considered a general lien.

A banker may use a general lien to retain stocks, bonds, or other papers that come into his possession from customers until all money owed by the customer is paid. A retail store that sells goods for a customer on commission may hold onto all goods entrusted to him until the owner pays any balance due on past commissions. The store may sell the remaining goods on hand to satisfy the general lien, but he must give the owner an accounting of the proceeds of a sale and return any excess profits realized by the sale to the owner. General liens are not used as often as specific liens.

Question 45. **What are real-property tax liens?**

A homeowner can end up with a real-property tax lien placed against his property by the city or county government if he fails to pay property taxes. The amount of the lien is based on the past-due taxes, as well as any interest and penalties.

If the lien is not paid in two to three years after your taxes are past due, the tax collector of the city or county can foreclose on the tax lien and sell the property at a tax deed sale. The county clerk will advertise a tax deed sale listing the properties that will be available for sale at least thirty days prior to the sale date. Most counties hold tax deed sales about once or twice a month.

Question 46. **What are federal tax liens?**

If you owe back taxes to the federal government and don't pay them after the IRS has demanded payment, the IRS can attach a federal tax lien to your property. In order to do this, the IRS must file a notice of federal tax lien at the office in the county or state where the property subject to the lien is located. The filing of a federal tax lien is the core of the type of collection action the IRS can take to recover back taxes.

Because the IRS is not required to notify or make a public announcement regarding the existence of a federal tax lien, this lien is sometimes known as the *secret lien* because it exists as a matter of law and can be perfected even without the filing of a notice. Tax liens usually have to be filed within two to three years of the due date of the taxes, and they expire after ten. The IRS can refile the lien within one year after the lien expires.

The federal government can foreclose on the lien and force the sale of the property. A federal tax lien does supersede state law, so any homestead or other protection provided in your state will not stand against a federal action. If the federal government does decide to foreclose on your property, the property owner will receive a notice of seizure, foreclosure, or auction.

If you see a federal tax lien on a piece of property you want to buy, be sure that lien is cleared before you purchase the property or that the lien is paid at closing. Then follow up with the county to be sure the lien is released against the property.

Question 47. **How can I have a federal tax lien removed from the property's title?**

In order to get a federal tax lien removed from a property, you must first either pay the back taxes, plus any penalties or interest, in full or work out a compromise agreement that includes the removal of the federal tax lien. If you are buying property with a federal tax lien against it, you should make sure the lien is removed before closing or that the payoff and proper legal filings will be done as a requirement of the closing. If property you want to buy is involved, your best bet is to work with an attorney on the removal of that tax lien.

Within thirty days after you pay off the IRS or have it adjusted, the IRS will submit a notice to the county to remove the tax lien. The IRS should file a certificate of release of federal tax lien with your county. If that is not done, you can call the IRS at 800-913-6050 for assistance. You may have to pay fees charged by your state or county in relation to the release of the lien.

Question 48. **What are mechanic's liens?**

Any time work is done on a home by a contractor, architect, surveyor, or mechanic, and the bill is not paid, a mechanic's lien can be filed against the property with a county clerk in the county where the property is located. This type of lien is a secured interest in the property. If the debt is not paid, the lien holder can foreclose on the property and force the sale of the property. After you've bought property and hired a contractor to fix it up, a mechanic's lien can be a problem as well.

Sometimes you hire a contractor to do work on the property, who then in turn hires subcontractors. You pay the contractor, but he does not pay his subcontractors. Any of the subcontractors or suppliers who weren't paid can place a mechanic's lien on your home. Be sure you know who did work on your home, and ask for a lien release from all potential lien claimants before you pay the contractor. You can find a good example of a lien release on the California Contractors State License Board (*www.cslb.ca.gov/forms/LienReleaseForms.pdf*).

A mechanic's lien is invalid unless it has been perfected (filed with the appropriate government office) and foreclosed on in the appropriate time. Typically, a lien must be filed within sixty or ninety days of the work's completion. The contractor then has one year to ask for a foreclosure and force the sale of the home to collect his debt.

If a mechanic's lien is placed on your home, contact an attorney to assess your options. In some cases, the lien may not be valid. For example, you might not have paid the contractor because the work is not yet done. An attorney can help you sort out the validity of the lien and work with you to get the lien released. The one thing you should never do is ignore the fact that a mechanic's lien has been placed on your home.

Question 49. **What are judgment liens?**

A judgment lien is one in which the court, through a court judgment, grants one of your creditors an interest in your property to satisfy a debt, such as the repayment of an award for damages. This debt can be based on your credit spending, but there are also numerous other reasons a judgment lien can be placed against your property.

For example, suppose while you were driving a car, you caused an accident in which the police determined you were at fault for causing injury to someone. The injured person could sue you. If he won the suit, a judgment lien could be placed against your property.

The lien holder could foreclose on your property and force a sale in order to collect his money if you don't pay voluntarily.

In many states, if you fail to replay the lien, the creditor can ask a court to issue a writ of execution, which will allow the county sheriff to seize and sell your property to pay the debt as well as any expenses of the sale. If a judgment lien is placed against your home, contact an attorney immediately to assess the situation and determine your options for protecting your home. A judgment lien usually has time limitations. Most judgment liens must be foreclosed on within ten to twenty years, or they expire.

Question 50. **What is a consensual lien?**

Any lien to which you voluntarily consent is called a consensual lien. The most common type of consensual lien is a mortgage. For example, as a homebuyer, you consent to give the bank a security interest in your home in exchange for the money you need to buy the home. This type of consensual lien is called a purchase-money security interest lien.

Another type of lien is called the non–purchase-money security interest lien. When you consent to this type of lien, it usually involves property you own that you use as collateral in exchange for a loan. Examples of this type of lien are a second mortgage or an equity line.

When you consent to both types of liens, they are usually considered non-possessory, which means as the debtor, you still own the property and it is titled in your name. But some consensual liens can be possessory. For example, if you pawn a watch in exchange for a loan from a pawnbroker, he will likely take possession of the watch until you repay the loan.

Question 51. **What are mortgage and deed-of-trust liens?**

You agree to a mortgage or deed-of-trust lien voluntarily when you buy a house, or other property, and pledge the property as security for the repayment of the debt. If you don't make the payments, the lender can foreclose on your security instrument, which is the mortgage or deed-of-trust lien.

Once he takes all the necessary steps to foreclose on the property, whether by judicial or nonjudicial means (read Chapter 2 for more information on this), the lender can then force a sale of your home in a public foreclosure auction or trustee's sale. The foreclosure process does vary by state. Chapter 12 covers the rules for each of the states.

Question 52. **What are state inheritance-tax liens?**

Many states levy an inheritance tax against the estates of a deceased person. If the money is not paid, the amount of the inheritance tax becomes a lien against the estate.

Some states do allow inheritance-tax exemptions, so tax rates can differ depending upon who receives the property. For example, a deceased spouse will likely be taxed at a lower rate than a friend of the deceased. Some states are starting to phase out state inheritance taxes.

If a state inheritance-tax lien is placed against a piece of property you own or plan to buy, the sale of the property can be forced by court order to pay the inheritance taxes.

Question 53. **What are corporate franchise tax liens?**

Some states collect corporate franchise taxes. This tax is imposed on corporations that want the right to conduct business within the state. If a corporation fails to pay its franchise tax, the state can file a lien against any real property in the state that belongs to the corporation.

Question 54. **What are bail-bond liens?**

If you or a family member needs to be bailed out of jail, and you put your house up for collateral, the bail company will likely place a bail-bond lien against your property. These liens are a type of insurance policy for the court. If the person doesn't show up in court, the amount of the bond is paid to the court, and a warrant is issued for the arrest of the person who didn't show up.

These liens are usually secured using a deed of trust, which enables the bail-bond company to foreclose on your property if the person who was bailed out of jail does not show up for court. The deed of trust will be recorded in the county where the property is located.

The bail-bond company can also foreclose on the property if the bond premium is not paid. Since the bond is similar to insurance, you will have bond premiums to pay plus any accrued interest. Most bail-bond premiums are for a period of one year. If the trial takes longer, then you would need to renew the premium for each year involved.

When the case finally ends, during the final court appearance, be sure the defendant's attorney asks for the court to release (exonerate) the bond. The bonding company won't remove the lien until the bond is exonerated and you have paid all premiums and any interest due. Once the court has ordered the bond exonerated and you have paid all premiums, the bail-bond company has thirty days to send you a *reconveyance,* which is a document that officially releases the lien against your property. Once you get that reconveyance, be sure you have it recorded with the county as well in order to clear your property title.

Question 55. **What are code-enforcement liens?**

If you get a notice from a local or county government agency that indicates that your property does not meet code, the government entity can fine you for not complying. If you fail to pay the fine, a code-enforcement lien can be placed against your property.

Several types of code-enforcement liens can be placed against your property, depending on the type of violation and the level of abatement required. The common types include the following:

- Notice of abatement proceedings: This type of lien does not specify the dollar amount required to remove the lien. This notice notifies prospective buyers or lenders that violations exist on the property.

- Partial abatement lien: After administrative abatement hearings, a hearing officer will order the property owner to correct a violation and will also assess payment to cover costs and penalties for failure to correct the code violation. This lien notifies the public of the violation and can prevent the sale or refinancing of the property. It sometimes can stop the owner from getting insurance on the property as well.
- Supplemental abatement lien: This lien is recorded when additional costs are incurred after the partial lien is recorded.
- Notice of lis pendens: This lien notifies the public that a lawsuit has been filed and is in addition to a partial abasement lien or notice of abatement proceedings.

Question 56. **What is a fraudulent lien?**

If someone files a lien against your property based on information that is not true, it is a fraudulent lien. A fraudulent lien is not enforceable. In fact, a lien holder who willfully exaggerates the amount claimed in a lien can be held responsible to the owner for all damages incurred because of the filing of the lien plus punitive damages. The filing of a fraudulent lien is a criminal offense that constitutes a felony in most states.

Question 57. **What is slander of title?**

If someone publishes false and malicious statements regarding your title to real estate, this could be considered a slander of title. To prove your case, you will need to prove the statement is false and that the statement was made with malicious intent. To collect damages, you will need to prove that the statement caused actual or special damages, which are damages that are a natural consequence of the slander, such as the salability or loss of use of the property.

For example, suppose a person deliberately states facts that are untrue about your house, and these statements result in the loss of a sale of your home. In order to win a slander of title case in court, you would need to prove that the facts were not true and the person acted maliciously. Your damages could include the expense of litigation as well as any loss incurred because the home sale did not occur as expected. You could also sue for punitive damages, which are intended to punish the offending party.

Question 58. **What are municipal liens?**

If you fail to pay for municipal services, such as water, sewage, or trash removal, your local government entity can place a municipal lien against your property for the money owed. Any lien imposed by the authority of a municipal government is a municipal lien.

Municipal liens are also used for major improvements done by the city or county. For example, suppose the city decides to put in new sidewalks. Each property in the area where the sidewalks are to be built may have a municipal lien placed against the property for its share of the costs. The lien is lifted when the county assessment is paid off in full by the homeowner.

Question 59. **What are welfare liens?**

If a homeowner collects welfare payments from state or federal government agencies and it is later determined that he was not legally entitled to those welfare payments, the government agency can file a welfare lien against his home.

The government entity can approve the sale of a home for the amount of the welfare lien. Whoever buys the home would have to satisfy any other liens, including the mortgage.

Question 60. **What are public defender liens?**

If a homeowner needed the services of a court-ordered public defender and was not able to pay for those services, a public-defender lien can be placed against the property by the local, state, or federal government. The judge of the circuit court or the magistrate judge sets the lien at a reasonable amount for the services rendered.

Question 61. **What are marital-support liens?**

If the court orders marital-support payments that a homeowner fails to make, a lien can be placed against the homeowner's property's title by the state and federal government. Foreclosure is not likely for the collection of a marital support lien, but having this type of lien placed against a property leads to trouble in its sale or transfer.

Question 62. **What are child-support liens?**

If a homeowner owes child support and doesn't pay it in full, the state or federal government can place a child-support lien against the property until the past-due child-support payments are made. In many states, these liens can be placed without an additional court hearing.

While foreclosure is not likely to satisfy a lien, the child-support lien must be paid in full when the property is sold or transferred. Failure to pay a child-support lien can stall the sale or transfer of property.

Question 63. **What are homeowners' association liens?**

If you own or plan to buy a piece of property that is located inside the boundaries of a homeowners' association, you will be required to pay fees to the homeowners' association. These fees are usually determined at annual meetings and assessed to each of the property owners to pay for upkeep, landscaping, roads, and other facilities offered by the association.

An association can place a homeowners' association lien against the property for any unpaid assessments. If a homeowner fails to pay, the association can foreclose on the property to collect the past-due payments.

If you are planning to buy a property located in a homeowners' association, be certain that the homeowner is current on his payments to the association. If not, you can get a surprise at closing and need to come up with a significant amount of cash unexpectedly.

Question 64. **What are subordinate lien holders?**

Subordinate lien holders include any person who holds a lien after the senior, or first, lien holder. In most cases, the senior lien holder is the lender who financed the initial purchase of the property and holds the first mortgage.

Subordinate lien holders would include a lender who offered you a second mortgage or equity line loan. Other subordinate lien holders would include holders of liens mentioned above.

The holder of the senior lien or first mortgage must be paid before subordinate lien holders can get their money. That is why, in most cases, if you apply for a second mortgage or equity loan, your interest rates are higher. The risk these lenders take is higher because they will only be paid after the first mortgage holder has been paid in full.

Question 65. **What is a junior lien holder?**

Any lien holder who filed a lien after the mortgage was executed is considered a junior lien holder. Essentially, the first person to record a lien is the senior lien holder, and all other lien holders are junior lien holders. If the property is foreclosed, the senior lien holder must be paid before the junior lien holders get anything. The junior lien holders are paid in the order in which their liens were filed with the county.

Question 66. **What is a senior lien holder?**

The senior lien holder is the lien holder that filed the first lien in the county where the property is located and has first priority to being paid if the property is foreclosed. In most cases, the senior lien holder is the bank that holds the first mortgage.

Question 67. **What is a lot-book report?**

A lot-book report is a limited report that includes all liens that have been recorded against the property. This includes all trusts, security interests, and other similar recorded documents that affect the property subject to the report. This is a limited report to give you some idea of the recent mortgage and deed-of-trust history, but it is not as comprehensive as a full title search. You won't be able to get title insurance with this type of report, but it could be useful to find out all current holders of mortgages or deeds of trust. The report should include maps that show the property's location and the layout of the parcel, as well as all owners on the title.

Chapter 4

BUYING A PROPERTY DURING THE LIS PENDENS PHASE

You can buy a property headed for foreclosure before the property goes to court for foreclosure. If you're in a state that requires all foreclosures to go through a court procedure then a lis pendens is filed. You can search your county records for lis pendens filings and find houses you may want to buy before the house goes to foreclosure.

Question 68. **What is lis pendens?**

Lis pendens is Latin for "a suit pending." This term can refer to any pending lawsuit. When it is filed concerning real estate, it indicates to any potential buyer or lender that there is a lawsuit pending involving the title to the property or a claim of ownership interest in the property.

This notice is filed with the county land-records office. The time period from when a lawsuit is filed until the time the case is actually heard in court is called *lis pendens*. Once the county records a lis pendens against a piece of property, all are alerted that the property's title is in question. This does make the property less attractive to some buyers and lenders, but if you are interested in buying pre-foreclosures, this gives you notice of a potential investment property.

Be careful, though. If you do decide to buy the property after the lis pendens is filed, you take that ownership of the property with the knowledge that it will be subject to the ultimate decision of the lawsuit. Only buy a piece of property after a lis pendens has been filed if you also know that the lawsuit is settled and the parties involved have been or will be satisfied as part of the expenses of the purchase of the property.

Question 69. **When does lis pendens begin?**

The lis pendens process begins when a lawsuit is filed against the property owner and a public notice of this suit is recorded against the property in the county where the property is located. The period of lis pendens continues until the case involved is heard in court.

Question 70. **What is posted as part of the lis pendens notice?**

The notice of lis pendens will show the court in which the lawsuit is filed. In addition, you will find the parties involved in the lawsuit, the case number, a legal description of the property, and the reason for the lawsuit. You will also find the date of the notice and the legal office that filed the notice.

Question 71. **How do you find lis pendens properties?**

Finding all lis pendens filings during a particular period of time is very simple in today's world of online record searching. You can go to the county clerk's Web site for the county in which you are interested in buying property and search the official records.

When you get to the official records search page, you'll need to put in a name. All you have to do is put in any letter of the alphabet, such as A, to get a listing of all lis pendens filings for people whose names start with A. Then you'll need to put in a code for the type of document you want to search. You should find a link to the code abbreviations right on the search page. Then you'll need to put in a date range for the search. You can then see the lis pendens notice online and find out whether or not it involves a homeowner and a mortgage company and if a foreclosure is involved.

Select the properties in neighborhoods that interest you. Then you can research further details by doing an official records search for the property and get more details about its appraised value, the amount of property taxes, and the status of tax payments.

Question 72. How do you convince an owner to sell during the lis pendens phase?

Your first contact with a property owner in the lis pendens phase should be by letter. In the letter, you should let the person know how you found out about the filing of a lawsuit to begin the foreclosure process. Briefly discuss the auction process and the fact the homeowner will get nothing from the auction sale. Discuss the time it would take to sell a home given current market conditions and how that may be not quick enough to meet the demands of the lender prior to the auction.

Tell the owner you specialize in helping people in the county facing foreclosure, and give a number to contact you regarding the help you offer. Indicate that you are interested in buying the home today and that you can give them a cashier's check for their house in as little as five days. (Be sure you do have the financing lined up to meet the promise you make in the letter.) Let them know that a sale of the home will stop the foreclosure and keep it off their credit report. Offer to help them find another place to live, and let them know you can handle all the details of the sale and work with their lender.

Be sure you send this letter by first class mail and indicate you want address services. You do that by printing "Address Service Requested" under your return address. That way the post office will return the mail to you with a correct address rather than forward on to the owner's new address if they've moved out of the home.

Make sure your letter looks professional and is personally addressed. Remember many people are doing the same thing as you in trying to make contact to buy the property prior to foreclosure. Most of these people will send a direct-mail piece that is not personal, often using a post card. You want your piece to look professional and personal to get the person to call you.

Don't try to cold-call the owner either by stopping at their home or making a phone call. They've probably already had many of those visits from strangers and will just ask you to leave or hang up on you. Few people will discuss the details of their finances with a stranger who just shows up at the door or calls on the phone.

If you don't hear from the person you've contacted by mail, don't hesitate to send a follow-up letter every couple of weeks indicating you are still interested in helping them and to please call. Track all letters that you've sent and set up a tickler file so you remember to send follow-up letters. Each letter you send should convey the sense of greater urgency to act to avoid foreclosure. Someone who calls in response to your letter and asks to meet with you will be much more responsive to what you have to say and much more likely to be ready to consider a deal.

Question 73. **How do you write a contract during the lis pendens phase?**

Don't try to write a contract for real estate in any phase of foreclosure without the help of a real estate attorney and a good title-search company. The laws in each state vary, and you don't want to get yourself locked into a contract that does not protect you from other creditors and liens. Before making an offer, be certain that you've had a thorough title search done and have found any potential claims against the property.

Your best bet is to find a good real estate attorney. Discuss your plans to buy foreclosures, let him tell you the possible pitfalls in your state and what you need to look for when researching potential properties. He will most likely have a basic contract form that you can use when negotiating with a buyer. Also, before writing the contract, be sure you have a copy of the mortgage estoppel letter (as described in question 29) to be sure you know the full financial details of the property in question. If you find during your research that the property owner has more than one lien against the property, you'll need to know the financial details for satisfying all liens so you can clear the title.

Question 74. **How do you close on a deal during the lis pendens phase?**

When a property owner has already reached the lis pendens phase, you can be certain that he has received numerous notices from the lender regarding his delinquency and the money owed to cure that delinquency. Get the contact information for the mortgage lender, as well as any other lenders or debtors who might have a lien on the property. Liens can be other mortgages (such as an equity line or a second mortgage), or they can be judgment or tax liens or many of the other kinds of liens discussed in Chapter 3. As part of the closing process, you will need to clear these liens to have a clean title and close on the loan.

Don't try to close on a property under the cloud of a lis pendens without the help of an attorney who can be sure that all the "I's" are dotted and the "T's" are crossed. The last thing you need to find out when you try to record the new title of ownership is that you can't record a clean title until an old lien on the property is satisfied. You'll be the one stuck with satisfying the lien.

Chapter 5

BUYING A PRE-FORECLOSURE

The best time to buy a foreclosure property is during the pre-fore-closure phase, before a property is put up for auction. These are usually the most motivated sellers, and your chances of making a purchase can be very good. When buying pre-foreclosures rather than foreclosure property at auction, your big advantage is that you can inspect the property prior to purchase. Unless you find a way to sweet-talk your way into a house owned by someone who's facing a foreclosure auction (and the chances of your being well received are slim), buying properties at auction can be very risky. You have no idea about the condition of the property and what you will find if you happen to win the bid. This chapter discusses pre-foreclosures and how you go about buying them.

Question 75. **What is a pre-foreclosure?**

When a property is said to be in pre-foreclosure, it means that the owner has received a notice of default or a lis pendens. The property is in pre-foreclosure until the date of the auction. If the property owner received a notice of default, the notice will include the date and time of the auction, which in most states is about ninety days later. For more information about the timing in your state, read Chapter 12. If a lawsuit has been filed, this means the property must go through a judicial foreclosure process, which probably will take even longer, before an auction date is set.

Question 76. **What are the benefits of buying a pre-foreclosure?**

You have two big advantages in buying a pre-foreclosure property rather than buying one at a foreclosure auction:

- The homeowner is likely desperate to sell and willing to settle for almost anything to avoid facing the actual foreclosure and destroying his credit history even more severely. While a foreclosure may not make it impossible to buy another property, a person with a foreclosure on his credit history will have a hard time finding a lender and will pay dearly in higher interest rates when he does find one.
- You will be able to inspect the property prior to purchasing and know exactly what levels of repairs are needed. If you buy at an auction, you never know what you are facing until after you've already made the purchase. Few people facing an auction on their property will let you inside prior to the day of auction.

Question 77. **What are the steps in buying a pre-foreclosure?**

Buying pre-foreclosures does require you to do your homework. You must like research and be very good at paying attention to detail. Here are the steps you'll need to take if you want to get into the business of buying pre-foreclosures:

- Find property owners who are facing default or foreclosure. Question 78 covers how to do that.
- Develop a set of letters that you can use to make initial contact with homeowners you've identified. Cold-calling in person or by phone will not work. By the time people reach the pre-foreclosure stage, you can be sure they are sick of answering the phone or door because they have been battered by collection people. They certainly won't give any financial information to a stranger who stops by or calls. Question 79 covers contact strategies in more detail.
- Research both the loan and the court records to identify all liens and the terms involved for paying off any liens and outstanding debt on the property. Questions 80 and 81 give more detail regarding research you should do.
- Do a careful inspection of the pre-foreclosure property. Inspection is covered in greater detail in question 82.
- After collecting all the financial information about paying off outstanding loans and satisfying liens against the property, as well as completing a careful inspection so you can estimate any repair costs you need to factor in to your decision-making process, you then must determine the market value of the foreclosure property and set a price you are willing to offer the property owner.
- Negotiate the price you set with the property owner. Question 83 covers negotiation strategies in greater detail.
- Negotiate with the foreclosing lender, as well as any subordinate lien holders. These negotiation strategies are covered in questions 84 and 85.
- Prepare a package for a short-sale. This process is covered in Chapter 6.
- Make a purchase offer. Question 86 covers protecting yourself regarding this situation.
- Close on the property. Possible pitfalls and how you can protect your rights are discussed in question 87.

Question 78. **How do you find property owners who are in default or facing foreclosure?**

Question 71 covers in detail how to go about doing an online search for lis pendens property. That is just one type of property in a pre-foreclosure state. You can use the same method of online search for other types of documents that would give you hints about whether or not a property is nearing foreclosure.

For example, you can search for documents such as notice of default, notice of foreclosure, notice of auction, tax liens, or any other document that would give you a clue that there may be financial stress creating a situation in which foreclosure could be possible. Not all bankruptcies and tax liens end in foreclosure, so if you use these codes to search, be sure to look for additional filings indicating possible foreclosure as you search for the properties that interest you. The counties in which you want to conduct the search will give you a list of documents and the codes you need to conduct this search.

You can also find pre-foreclosure properties by reading the newspaper where foreclosure notices are printed. While this will give you good leads, they likely will be much later in the process. Conducting an online search once a week will give you a jump on others seeking to buy foreclosures because you will find out within a week or two of when the lender started the three- to four-month process toward foreclosure. As a result, you'll have more time to try to make contact with the homeowner.

Question 79. **How do you contact property owners in default or facing foreclosure?**

You should always make initial contact with the homeowner by direct mail. Remember these homeowners have already been hounded by telephone by creditors and are very unlikely to talk with a stranger by phone or one who tries to solicit them by just stopping by.

Write a professional letter, and let the homeowners know how you found out about the property by indicating the public filing you used. Tell the homeowners about the auction process and that they will get nothing from the auction sale. Discuss the current real estate market and how long it would take for them to sell a home. Remind them that this may not be fast enough to stop the foreclosure.

Tell them you specialize in helping people who are facing foreclosure, and give them a number where they can contact you regarding your help. Let them know you are interested in buying their home today and that you can give them a cashier's check for their house in as little as five days. (Be sure you do have the financing lined up to meet the promise you make in the letter.) Let them know that a sale of the home will stop the foreclosure and keep it off their credit report. Offer to help them find another place to live, and let them know you can handle all the details of the sale and work with their lender.

Be sure you send this letter by first-class mail and indicate you want address services. You do that by printing "Address Service Requested" under your return address. That way the post office will return the mail to you with a correct address rather than forward on to the owner's new address if they've moved out of the home.

Make sure your letter looks professional and that it looks as though it was personally addressed, even if you use a printer to address your letters. Remember many other people are also trying to make contact to buy properties prior to foreclosure. Most of these people send a direct-mail piece that is not personal, often using a post card. You want your piece to look professional and personal to get the person's attention and get you in the door.

Don't expect to get a call after the first letter is sent. While it does happen, that will be a rare response. Expect to send at least two to three letters before you hear from someone. It's best to send your letters about two weeks apart. Each letter should sound a bit more urgent as the person nears the actual foreclosure.

Question 80. **How do you verify loan information for loans in default?**

You can get the information regarding the loan in default by asking the homeowner to request a mortgage estoppel letter (as described in question 29) from the lender's loss-mitigation department. This letter will let you know if the loan is a DHA, FHA, conventional, or private loan. You'll also get details about the principal loan balance, interest rate, months remaining on the loan, and total monthly payment. You should also look for any accrued interest, late payment charges, legal costs, and past-due loan payments so you know the total amount needed to cure the loan.

Having the homeowner request the mortgage estoppel letter is the best and fastest way to get the information. If the homeowner doesn't have this information, you can help him get it from the lender.

Question 81. **What type of research is necessary before buying a pre-foreclosure?**

In addition to finding out the details about the mortgage in default, you also must search the title to the property to find out if there are any other loans and liens. Chapter 3 covers all the possible liens that a property might have. These liens will have to be cleared before a property can be sold.

You also want to be certain that you are in contact with all owners of the property, and that means you need to research who holds title. If it's more than the one person, you will need to make contact with everyone, even if they are not on the mortgage involved. For example, if there was a divorce but the ex-spouse is still on the title but the homeowner is unwilling to make contact, you will need to contact the ex-spouse and get him to agree to the sale.

To be sure you do get all the information you need, hire a person who specializes in title searches. That may cost you $200 to $300, but it's a lot better than paying off a $25,000 lien that you did not find on your own.

It can't hurt to do a search using Google or other search engine to find out more about the homeowner. You may find out something you can use that will have you negotiate for the property, or you may find out something about the person's criminal past that will make you decide to pass on that property.

One last thing you want to do before making an offer on the property is to contact your insurance agent and ask him to check the claims history for the property. You agent can tell you if there is a significant claims problem and whether the property will be insurable.

Question 82. **How do you inspect a pre-foreclosure property?**

The big advantage of buying pre-foreclosure property is that you can inspect the property before buying it, so be sure you do that inspection. Even if you consider yourself a pro at home repairs, don't get cheap. Pay a professional property inspector who knows the neighborhood and is aware of the common problems found in homes in that neighborhood.

You should include a clause that permits you to inspect the property in the contract for any real estate property you plan to buy, whether or not it is a foreclosure. This clause should also include your right to rescind the offer if after the inspection you decide that more repairs are necessary than you want to make.

Also, don't forget to check out the neighborhood if you are not familiar with the area. After you get the property ready for sale, you want to be able to sell it. So take a walk around the neighborhood and look for any problems that might make it difficult to sell the home. These include drainage or flooding problems (best to check the area after a heavy rain or talk with the neighbors), noisy neighbors, and signs of drugs or drinking in the area. It's also a good idea to drive by the property at night. Some neighborhoods that look quiet and peaceful during the day turn into dangerous places at night.

Question 83. **How do you negotiate with owners of the pre-foreclosure property?**

After you done a thorough job of researching the property, the title, and any liens and mortgages, as well as completing a thorough inspection of the property, you're ready to decide whether or not to make an offer on the property. Use the details you've collected about the property, as well as details about home sales in the area, to come up with an offer price. Be sure to consider the cost of repairs when calculating that price. You should start the negotiations by offering to buy the property at about 40 to 45 cents on the dollar based on current market value in the area. You may want to start higher if the property is in a very desirable area and in excellent condition, but that combination is hard to find.

Be ready for a lot of owner resistance to selling the home. Most people facing foreclosure have done everything they can to try to stay in their home, so it will take some careful negotiation to even get them ready to accept an offer. You need to build trust with the owner and be careful not to be abrasive. Few people will sell to someone they dislike.

When you are ready to make the offer, be sure to negotiate directly with the owner. He may insist that you talk to his attorney or accountant, but tell him that he must be present for the negotiations even if a third party will handle them.

Question 84. **How do you negotiate with subordinate lien holders?**

In addition to negotiating with homeowners, you'll also have to negotiate with lien holders. Once you've got a contract in place, your next step is to talk with the subordinate lien holders. Lien holders that are subordinate to the senior mortgage should know that they won't get much, if anything, if the property goes to auction. Your goal will be to get lien holders with a valid lien to accept 50 percent or less on the value of their lien. You also will need to get any invalid or fraudulent liens cleared from the title as well.

Chapter 3 covers liens in more detail, including how to get them cleared.

You will ultimately have to pay off liens at closing to clear the title, or the lien will remain attached to the property after closing. The most common types of liens are second and third mortgages; deed-of-trust liens; judgment liens; mechanic's liens; state and federal welfare, medical, and child-support and welfare liens; and local, state, and federal tax liens.

When you call to talk with subordinate lien holders, your goal will be to convince them that it is much better to accept fifty cents on the dollar than to have their lien wiped out at a foreclosure auction. By accepting the lower payment at closing, lien holders at least get something. Your attorney who handles the closing can prepare whatever documentation is needed to clear the lien with the county clerk. Before paying the subordinate lien holder, be sure the needed documentation has been signed. If you find a lien holder that won't agree to your offer, you can offer more, pay the full price of the lien, or walk away from the purchase of the property.

Question 85. **How do you negotiate with foreclosing lenders or their representatives?**

You will need to work with the lender's loss-mitigation department in order to close the loan, especially if you want to negotiate a short-sale (covered in Chapter 6). If the lender says it doesn't have such a department, you may find that they call the same type of department by another name, such as default management department, loan workout department, loan resolution department, nonperforming assets department, foreclosure department, collections department, or special loans department. You should find the proper contact person on the documentation about the loan that you got from the homeowner during the investigation process.

Before trying to contact the lender, be sure you have an authorization letter from the mortgagor or trustor. Banks will not give out information without authorization from their customer. Tell the lender's representative you are ready to buy the property and help them get the property back on the books and generating income. You can add a sense of urgency to the conversation by telling the lender the owner is considering bankruptcy if the lender isn't willing to work out a deal. Tell them you have a strong credit history and the cash to make the sale possible today. Banks don't want to go to foreclosure and take over the property, so if you are making a reasonable offer, you have a good chance of getting the property, even if the offer is below the current mortgage balance. Once you convey to the loss-mitigation department that you are serious about buying the property and how quickly you can make it happen, ask the lender to overnight a loan reinstatement package that includes all details about the total amount needed to close the loan.

Question 86. How do you write a contract for a pre-foreclosure property?

Don't try to write a contract for real estate in any phase of foreclosure without the help of a real estate attorney and a good title search company. The laws in each state vary, and you don't want to get yourself locked into a contract that does not protect you from other creditors and liens. Before making an offer, be certain that you've had a thorough title search done and have found any potential claims against the property.

Your best bet is to find a good real estate attorney and discuss your plans to buy foreclosures. Let him tell you the possible pitfalls in your state and what you need to look for when researching potential properties in your state. He will most likely have a basic contract form that you can use when negotiating with a buyer. Also, before writing the contract, be sure you that have a copy of the mortgage estoppel letter (as described in question 29) to be sure you know the full financial details about the property in question. If you find during your research that the property owner has more than one lien against the property, you'll need to know the financial details for satisfying all liens so you can clear the title.

Question 87. **How do you close on a pre-foreclosure property?**

When a property owner has already reached the pre-foreclosure phase, you can be certain that the owner has received numerous notices from the lender regarding the delinquency and the money owed to cure it. Get the contact information for the mortgage lender, as well as any other lenders or debtors who might have a lien on the property. Liens can be other mortgages (such as an equity line or a second mortgage), or they can be judgment or tax liens or many of the other kinds of liens discussed in Chapter 3. As part of the closing process, you will need to clear these liens to have a clean title and close on the loan.

Be sure your attorney is aware that the property you want to close on is a foreclosure property. His staff will be on the alert for the types of problems likely when a homeowner is nearing foreclosure and make sure you get a clean title at closing.

Chapter **6**

BUYING A PROPERTY USING A SHORT-PAYOFF SALE

As a property gets closer and closer to foreclosure, you do have a greater and greater chance of clearing the senior mortgage for less than the amount due. This is called a short-payoff sale, but is more commonly known as a short-sale. This chapter explains a short-payoff sale and how it works.

Question 88. **What is a short-sale?**

When homeowners suffer a long-term financial hardship, during which time they can't maintain their mortgage loan, or if the property is nearing foreclosure, you may be able to negotiate with the lender for a short-sale. In this case, the loss-mitigation specialist may allow you to pay off less than the amount due on the mortgage. This is a short or pre-foreclosure sale, but is commonly called a short-sale. A homeowner must have identified a qualified buyer to use this option. That's where you come in. As a qualified buyer, you can make the discussion happen with the lender.

In addition to financial hardship, the property's physical condition and local real estate market conditions will become a factor. For example, if the property needs a lot of work before it can be sold, it will be easier to work out a short-sale. Also, if the real estate market is weak and it could take a long time to sell the home, the bank will probably be more willing to consider accepting less than the loan balance. It will be up to you to convince the bank that these conditions do exist.

Question 89. **Who is involved in a short-sale?**

You will find that three or four parties are involved in negotiating a short-sale. You and the homeowner are two of them. The lender (or investor) or whoever owns the loan will the third party.

Many lenders or investors also have a third party actually servicing the loan. (Chapter 7 discusses servicing lenders.) Whether you are working with the servicing lender or the original lender, you will need to contact the loss-mitigation department to work out the short-sale.

Question 90. **What is a loan loss-mitigation department?**

The loan loss-mitigation department is the department that will be responsible for working with a homeowner whose mortgage loan is in default. You may find that the lender calls this department something else, such as default management, loan workout, loan resolution, nonperforming assets, foreclosure, collections, or special loans. The name doesn't matter; all these departments do the same thing. This department is the one you'll need to work with to arrange a short-sale.

Loss-mitigation programs were created jointly by the federal government and the mortgage industry to come up with alternatives and stop home foreclosures. Short-sales are not the only option for a homeowner in financial trouble, and the loan loss-mitigation department is the one that tries to find the best solution to mitigate the lender's loss.

Question 91. **What is repaired value?**

The repaired value of a property is the value of the property after all repairs are completed. This is one of the factors the loan loss-mitigation department will consider when determining whether or not to accept a short-payoff offer. If the bank believes it can do the repairs and quickly sell the property for more than you are offering, it likely will not accept the short-sale.

You will need to make a strong case for your offer and carefully document the repairs needed and the cost of those repairs. Don't fudge. The bank will likely send out someone to appraise the property and make an independent determination.

Question 92. **In what types of situations would a lender consider a short-sale?**

Short-sales are usually a lender's last resort before proceeding with a foreclosure. You are more likely to be successful with this strategy if the lender knows he will have a difficult time selling the property should he take possession after a foreclosure.

These situations are most likely ones in which the lender will consider a short-sale:

- The house was bought or refinanced at the top of a seller's market at an inflated price.
- The property was refinanced at 125 percent of its value, which was based on an inflated property-appraisal report.
- Property values have dropped significantly due to economic conditions.
- The property value of the home dropped below the amount of the loan balance.

- The property's "as is" condition is so bad the lender would not be able to sell it after a foreclosure.

Question 93. **What would a lender consider a "short-sale"?**

Any payoff that is less than the total balance due, including all past-due payments, all accrued interest, all legal fees and administrative costs, as well as the principal due on the mortgage, would be consider a short-sale.

Question 94. **How does a lender's financial condition impact its consideration of a short-sale?**

The lender's financial position can influence whether or not it will accept a short-sale. Some key financial factors that might make it easier for you to get approval for a short-sale include these:

- The number of nonperforming loans on the books
- The lender's weak overall financial condition
- If a third-party investor who owns the loan is looking to reduce the number of risky loans he holds
- Weak real estate market conditions, in which the lender knows it will have a hard time selling a foreclosed property or it will need to pay carrying costs for a long time before the property is sold

Question 95. **How do borrowers qualify for a short-sale?**

Borrowers must pass a hardship test to qualify for a short-sale. Each lender will have its own set of guidelines for the hardship test, but here are the most common conditions a lender will consider. A buyer will need to meet one or more of these conditions:

- The borrower or an immediate family member experienced a catastrophic illness that destroyed his financial position.
- The borrower's spouse died or the couple divorced, and the borrower does not have sufficient income to make the mortgage payments.
- The borrower was transferred by his employer and can't sell the home.
- The borrower was called to active military duty for an extended period and can't make the mortgage payments.
- The borrower suffered a disabling illness or injury and can't work again.
- The borrower lost his job and has no chance to get a job given current economic conditions.
- The borrower is financially insolvent and there is no expectation for his financial situation to turn around in the near future.
- The borrower is in jail and doesn't have the income to make the mortgage payments.

Question 96. What factors do lenders consider as part of the short-sale?

Lenders consider a number of factors when determining whether or not to agree to a short-sale, including these:

- The financial condition of the borrower
- The property's "as is" value
- The cost of putting the property into resale condition
- The property's value after repair
- The cost of securing and maintaining the property while it is being marketed for sale
- The cost of marketing and selling the property

In addition to factors involving the borrower and the condition of the property, other factors that must be considered include the financial condition of the lender or the third-party investor on the mortgage, the loss-mitigation policies of the lender and any investors, the procedures of any government agency insuring the loan (if applicable), and the number of the lender's underperforming loans.

Question 97. In what ways does private mortgage insurance impact the short-sale?

Private mortgage insurance (PMI) companies are the ones who will have to pay any shortfall, so if there is private mortgage insurance involved, expect to have more of a fight to get approval for the short-sale. PMI is required by a lender for any conventional mortgage loan in which the homebuyer put down less than 20 percent.

If the lender declares the loan in default, an insurer may help the borrower by coming up with the funds needed to cure the default and reinstate the loan. In some cases, the insurer may even purchase the loan from the lender and modify the repayment terms to make it easier for the borrower to stay in the home. If your offer requires a larger payment from the PMI insurer than would be necessary if it helped cure the loan, the insurer may try to make a different deal with the homeowner and possibly even buy the mortgage itself.

Question 98. How do you determine if a property might be eligible for a short-sale?

You will find that only a very small number of properties in foreclosure can make it through all the hoops required to qualify for a short-sale. Before you go through the work of trying to negotiate a short-sale, be sure you know the following:

- The total amount of liens against the property
- The lender's loan loss-mitigation policies
- Borrower's current financial condition and whether or not the borrower can pass the hardship test

- Current status and type of loan in default. (An FHA or VA loan faces very different conditions for negotiating an offer below the principal amount due. They also are set up with more options that allow a person in financial trouble to keep their home. See question 113 for more information about FHA loans and question 114 for more information about VA loans.)
- Property's as-is market value
- Property's as-repaired value
- Local economic and real estate market conditions

You will need to know all these factors to make your case for a short-sale effectively. If the borrower does not meet the hardship requirements, don't even bother trying to put together a short-payoff proposal. It won't fly.

Question 99. **Who gives final approval for a short-sale?**

The final approval for a short-sale must come from the investor that owns the loan. If you are working with a servicing lender, you will need to plan for at least thirty extra days, and it could be as long as ninety days to get approval from the lender who owns the loan.

Question 100. **How do you get approval for a short-sale?**

You must jump through a lot of hoops to get approval for a short-payoff sale. The most important factor is that you must have the cash to close the deal. All short-sales must be closed with cash.

If you do have the cash on hand (or have worked out financing so you can bring cash to the table), your next step is to get a written authorization from the borrower to release loan information to you. When the lender gets this letter, he will send a short-sale package that lists all the requirements.

You will then have to prepare a short-sale proposal letter (as described in question 101) and attach a HUD 1 Settlement

Statement that shows how much money the lender will net from the sale. The settlement sheet must show that the borrower is getting $0. The lender will not approve a short-sale if the borrower will get money from the deal.

You will need to include the borrower's short-sale application (as described in question 103), a statement about the current real estate market conditions, a listing of all repairs that are needed, and pictures of the current as-is condition of the property.

In addition to this information, you should be sure to provide anything else that the lender requests in the short-sale package, which must include a signed purchase agreement for the property. When the lender gets the package, he will order a broker's appraisal report for the property showing the as-is and as-repaired prices for the property.

After all is received, the lender will then make a decision about whether or not to accept the short-sale. If the sale is refused, the buyer of the property can make a counteroffer, which will then be accepted or refused. If an offer is accepted, the buyer will close the sale within thirty days.

Question 101. **What is a short-sale proposal letter?**

The short-sale proposal letter summarizes the key parts of your offer to purchase the property. You should include the price you are willing to pay and a few key points about how you arrived at that price. Be sure to mention real estate market conditions and to attach comparable listings near the property address. You should state the amount you've gotten in bids for home repairs and attach as part of the package copies of these repair costs estimates.

If property values have been declining over the past couple of years, state that and offer proof of that statement in the package. You do want to indicate the borrower is insolvent.

Be sure that your short-sale package matches the statements that you make in the proposal letter.

Question 102. **What is a "borrower's authorization to release information"?**

The borrower's authorization to release information is a short letter to the lender giving it permission to release details about the loan to the party specified in the letter. A lender cannot discuss the details of a person's account until they have this letter on file.

Question 103. **What is a borrower's short-sale application?**

Borrowers must provide substantial details about their financial position and the hardship factors involved in their seeking a short-sale. These pieces of information include the following:

- Hardship letter
- Financial history
- Payroll check stubs from the borrower's employer (if employed)
- Financial history
- Tax returns for the past two years
- Bank statements for the past six months
- Check stubs from unemployment compensation (if receiving compensation)
- Copies of consumer credit files from the three key reporting agencies (Equifax, Experian, and Trans Union)
- Copies of any divorce decree and any obligations for child support and alimony

The lender may require other pieces of information. If so, the requirement will be stated in the paperwork package sent by the loss-mitigation department.

Question 104. **What is the borrower's financial statement?**

The borrower's financial statement must clearly spell out all assets the borrower owns and all liabilities the borrower owes to others. The loss-mitigation department will be looking for proof that the borrower is insolvent.

Question 105. **What must the borrower supply regarding his financial history?**

To back the financial statement, the borrower will need to provide proof of his financial condition. He will need to send bank statements for the past six months, check stubs of his paychecks, unemployment check stubs if those are appropriate, welfare payments, food stamp payments, and proof of any other types of income he or she receives, such as child support or alimony. In addition, he will need to supply current credit reports from the three key credit reporting agencies (Equifax, Experian, and Trans Union). If a medical illness is a factor in the financial hardship, then the borrower should include copies of medical bills.

The primary purpose of sending as much financial detail as possible is that the stronger the case made for financial hardship, the better the chance a lender will accept a short-payoff offer.

Question 106. **What are market comparables, and should you provide them?**

Market comparables include current real estate listings for properties that are comparable. That means property in approximately the same area and with the same number of rooms, bathrooms, basement or not and so on. If the market has been gradually declining over the past two years, then your market comparables should show the decline in real estate value as well.

Yes, you definitely should send market comparables. It will help you to make a strong case for the price you are offering, especially if the market is plummeting or houses are sitting on the market for a long time.

Question 107. How can you get the lender to pay repair costs?

While it's not likely that you will get help with the repair costs, it's certainly worth a try if there are significant repairs to be done. These repair costs can be submitted to the lender as part of the short-payoff offer, or they can be negotiated with the servicing lender or the homeowner's insurance company. The homeowner's insurance company may be willing to foot some of the bill if the homeowner can prove that the repairs are the result of an insurable loss.

Question 108. How much cash do you need to finance a short-sale transaction?

You will need to provide a verifiable proof of funds letter that indicates the source of funds needed to purchase the property when your proposal is for a short-sale. Chapter 11 discusses funding a foreclosure purchase in greater detail.

Question 109. Who is and is not eligible to buy a pre-foreclosure property as a short-payoff transaction?

You must be able to prove that you have no relationship to the borrower in order to get approval for a short-sale. You cannot be a family member, relative, or close friend to qualify as a buyer. The lender may actually file suit to rescind the sale if it finds out that the buyer was a relative or close friend who actually bought the property and then allowed the defaulting borrower to stay in the house.

Question 110. **Why are property owners reluctant to accept a short-sale?**

While a borrower you approach may at first be delighted to get the monkey off his back with a fast sale, the short-sale may not be as attractive as it first looks when you approached him. The two key reasons the owners may balk after initially sounding as though they may accept a short-sale include these:

- The borrower expected to receive proceeds from the sale, and the lender does not allow that to happen. Lenders usually will not agree to a short-sale if the borrower stands to get some cash from the sale because they do not want to reward borrowers who were financially irresponsible and are facing foreclosure.
- The borrower will face a tax burden after a short-sale. (See question 111 for more details about the taxes due.)

Question 111. **What are the tax consequences of a short-sale?**

When a borrower gets a lender to agree to a short-sale, he will have to consider any money saved as earned income. The IRS will charge federal income tax on the money saved as part of the short sale. For example, if the borrower owed $150,000 and the lender agrees to accept $120,000, the $30,000 saved will be considered the same as earned income. Even though the borrower gets no cash, he'll still have to pay taxes as though he earned income.

Question 112. **How is the value of the property determined in a short-sale transaction?**

The lender will determine the property value based on one or two appraisals from real estate brokers. The brokers will provide an as-is and as-repaired value for the property.

Question 113. **What are the unique provisions of a short-payoff transaction if it is an FHA property?**

FHA short-sales are called pre-foreclosure sales. In order for a lender to authorize a pre-foreclosure sale of an FHA-insured property, the lender must be an approved loss-mitigation lender for the U.S. Housing and Urban Development Department (HUD).

For an FHA borrower to be eligible for a pre-foreclosure sale, he must meet these criteria:

- The property must be occupied by the borrower.
- The loan must be at least ninety days late.
- The borrower must prove he meets the hardship test.
- The borrower must receive counseling from a HUD-approved agency prior to the proposal for a pre-foreclosure sale.

Question 114. **What are the unique provisions of a short-sale if it is a VA property?**

If the borrower is a veteran who got his loan through the U.S. Department of Veterans Affairs, you may be able to work out a compromise sale. This is the VA's version of a short-sale. A compromise sale is approved if the VA considers a loan in default to be impossible to fix after reviewing the borrower's financial condition. The borrower would have to be in a situation where he cannot prevent the foreclosure of his property and provide for his family.

Chapter 7

BUYING A PROPERTY DURING A FORECLOSURE SALE

While it's much better to buy a property in the pre-foreclosure phase—read Chapter 5 to find out why—you can be successful buying foreclosure properties at auction. You likely will not be able to see the inside of the property prior to the auction, but you can visit the property to see the outside. This chapter discusses the process of foreclosure sales and how you can be successful buying a property at a foreclosure auction.

Question 115. What is a public foreclosure auction?

After the lender has jumped through all the hoops required to foreclose on a property, the home will be sold at a public foreclosure auction. Potential buyers will bid on the property in a competitive bidding process. The highest bidder, as long as he bids the minimum amount required by the lender, will win the auction.

Buyers often must pay cash at the auction and frequently don't have much time to research the title or the condition of the property. You will not have to deal with the person being foreclosed upon at all through this process.

After the sale is complete, in many states, the buyer sends a legal notice and asks the former homeowner to vacate the premises in seventy-two hours. If the former homeowner does not vacate the property, the new owner can ask a judge to evict him. If you want to do so, you can accept rent from the former owner to give him a bit more time before having to move. The former owner does have the right to appeal the eviction decision within ten days.

Question 116. How do you find properties to be auctioned?

Information about the foreclosure sale will be published once a week for at least three successive calendar weeks before the date of the foreclosure sale in most states. The publication chosen for this notice must have general circulation in the county or counties in which the property in question is located.

The newspaper chosen will be conducive to providing notice of foreclosure to interested parties. For example, a newspaper that is generally accepted as the newspaper of legal record for the county or counties in which the property to be sold is located would be considered an appropriate newspaper. Your attorney will know which newspaper is likely to be used.

If there is no newspaper appropriate for this circulation, then a notice of default or foreclosure will be posted at the courthouse of the county or counties in which the property is located and at the place where the property sale will be held.

You can simplify the process of finding properties if you want to pay for the information. Two of the online sources that offer access to foreclosure information for a fee are *www.foreclosurenet.net* and *www.realtytrac.com*.

Question 117. **What is an "as is" sale?**

All foreclosure sales are "as is" sales, which means the buyer must take the property in its current state and cannot ask the current owner, often the bank, to do any repairs. In fact, a foreclosure property may not even be in insurable condition when the buyer completes the sale.

If the property is run down, an insurer can refuse to insure the property until repairs are completed. In addition, the buyer may not be able to insure the property title as title insurers are usually cautious about insuring foreclosed property. If some mistake was made by the lender or someone else during the foreclosure process, a court could rule that the sale was flawed, which means the property could be tied up in legal proceedings for months or even years.

Question 118. **How do you research a property before auction?**

Your first stop for researching a property before an auction should be the county clerk's office for the county in which the property is located. The information included in the auction notice should give you the street address and the legal description of the property, as well as its land use or zoning code. You should also find the tax assessed value, the original loan amount, the date the loan was made, the date of the last payment, and the total amount past due. You will also find the loan balance at the time the foreclosure action was filed.

These details will give you a starting point for your research. You should then research the title to see if there are any other mortgages or liens on the property. To be safe, you should contact a title company and find out what they would charge for a simple title search. While a full-blown search could cost $300, you may be able to save money by asking for a lot-book report (as described in question 67) for as little as $25 to be sure you don't miss any liens. If you do and they're not wiped out by the foreclosure, you could end up having to pay them off.

In addition, you should check out the property by driving by to see its exterior condition, as well as the condition of properties in the neighborhood. You won't be able to go inside, but you can walk around the neighborhood and possibly find neighbors who have been in the house and who can give you some information about the condition of the property.

Question 119. **How do you know what to bid?**

In the published notice, you will be able to find out the outstanding balance of the loan. In most cases, the lender who foreclosed on the property will bid at least that much on the house to be sure it gets its investment covered. Don't expect to get the house for less than the balance due on the mortgage, but if you don't think the house is worth that price, then you can bid lower.

As you review the lot-book report, note if there are any liens or mortgages senior to the one being foreclosed. For example, if the second mortgage holder is foreclosing, you will have to pay off the first mortgage holder as well to get a clean title. The foreclosure will wipe out any liens junior to the debt being foreclosed, but all senior debt must still be paid. You must include that debt in your calculation of what the purchase of the property will cost you. For example, if the amount due on the second mortgage is $50,000 and you can buy the property at auction for $60,000, but you still have to pay off the first mortgage at $100,000, then the total cost to you would be $160,000. If you think you could only sell the house for $170,000, then you should walk away from the deal. Most likely there are repairs to be done, and by the time you include your costs for selling the home, you likely won't make enough money to make the deal worthwhile.

Market conditions and the number of people bidding on the property will determine the ultimate price. The highest bidder is the one that will win the property. Don't get caught up in the excitement of the auction. Make a realistic estimate of what you think the property is worth, and guesstimate the repairs you think will be needed. Then determine the price you think you could get for the property after you fix it up. Figure in some profit for yourself, and come up with the maximum amount you want to offer for the property. Stop bidding when the auction price tops your maximum.

Question 120. **How do you assess the condition of the property?**

You won't be able to inspect the property, so you must be creative about how you can find out information about the property. You can get in trouble for trespassing, so don't try to enter the property, even the back yard, without permission. Homeowners facing foreclosure can be very nasty to anyone coming near their property.

Walk around the property on its legal boundaries and talk with the neighbors. Often neighbors have been inside the property fairly recently and can give you an idea of the condition of the property inside.

Question 121. **How do you research the title before the auction?**

You can research the title yourself at the county clerk's office in the county in which the property is located. There you should be able to find all mortgages and liens filed against the property. To be sure you haven't missed anything, you should contact a title company and find out its price for doing a lot-book report (described in question 67). That's a search that will list all existing liens, but it will not be as complete as a full title search going back in history to the time when the property was first owned.

You may also want to request a judgment lien report from the county clerk to be sure you don't miss any money judgments against the property. The judgment lien report will include all civil lawsuit judgments, state income tax liens, tax liens, personal property taxes, and family court matters, such as alimony or child-support liens.

Question 122. **What is the auction process?**

The opening bid for the property will be based on the total amount owed to the foreclosing lender, any interest incurred, late charges, penalties, any liens placed on the property by other institutions, and any fees incurred during the foreclosure process. If no one bids higher than the opening bid, the lender will get the property.

Question 123. **What can you learn by observing auctions before bidding yourself?**

Each state has its own bidding procedures. Your best way to find out how an auction is run in your state is to attend one or two auctions and just observe the process. You should never walk into an auction and start bidding unless you've observed a previous auction, you know how the auctioneer conducts the auction, and you know the rules in your state for bidding.

Some states require you to immediately have the cash or cashier's check to pay for the property at auction. Other states require that you bring a certain percentage of the winning bid price to the auction in cash. You then have thirty to ninety days to come up with the rest of the money.

Question 124. **Who conducts the foreclosure sale?**

In most states a foreclosure sale is conducted by a trustee, who is usually someone from the title insurance company, but a private individual can conduct the sale. Sometimes a lender will specify an auctioneer as part of the deed of trust or mortgage.

Question 125. **How do you bid?**

Most bids will be accepted at the auction, but in some states bidders can submit a written bid for the property prior to the auction. You will need to show that you have the funds necessary to pay at least the opening bid. Some trustees will permit you to pay only a percentage of the final bid, with the balance to be paid in thirty days. If you want to pay only a percentage of the bid at auction, you will need to contact the trustee prior to the auction and make arrangements for this credit bid (as discussed in question 128).

If written bids are submitted, they will be reviewed after all bids have been taken from the floor. If a written bid is higher than any bid at the auction, the person offering the written bid will win. The written bid must include a cashier's check for the minimum amount required in that state.

Question 126. **What is a bidding ring?**

You must be watchful at an auction for a piece of property that interests you. Sometimes shills will bid on the property who have no interest in buying but are trying instead to increase the price. This is called a *bidding ring*. Basically, members of such a ring want to get all newcomers out of the auction as quickly as possible by getting them caught up in auction fever, so they'll spend too much on one property and then leave. Often a bidding ring will include three or four people who frequent auctions. They divvy up the properties amongst themselves that they are interested in prior to the auction and then make sure each person in the ring gets the properties they want. While this is illegal, it does happen, so watch for it. If you do attend one or two auctions before the one you actually bid at, you will likely be able to observe if there is a bidding ring.

Question 127. **How do I prevent "auction fever"?**

Auctions can be exciting, and everyone can get caught up in the emotional whirlwind. Bidders become competitive and want to beat their competition. When this happens, you can get into a mentality in which you want to win at any cost—even if the price is well above what you thought was reasonable for the property.

Set a firm price you are willing to pay for the property, and don't bid above it. When you are at an auction, you can get caught up in auction fever and not even know. You may want to impress someone who's watching or may just feel the pressure of responding in time. Determine your maximum price prior to arriving at the auction and stop bidding when that price is exceeded.

Question 128. **What is a credit bid?**

Some states allow you to bid on credit by depositing a specified amount prior to the auction. Within ten days after the sale, the purchaser must pay the amount due plus any costs accrued since the auction sale. These additional costs can include interest on money-judgments loans. All money due must be paid before the credit bidder can get possession of the property. The amount of the credit bid on deposit prior to the auction will be forfeited if the winning bidder does not pay the total due within ten days of the sale.

Question 129. **What is a winning bid?**

The winning bid is the highest bid for the property. If, after the auction is closed, the bidder is not able to come up with the required cash, the winning bidder is the next-highest bidder.

Question 130. **What is the right to redeem?**

In twenty-five states, the borrowers and any creditors with a stake in the property have the right to redeem the property, which means to buy it back after the foreclosure sale. The rules vary state by state:

- Some states allow 365 days for the redemption period. These include Alabama, Idaho, Kansas, Kentucky, and Missouri.

- Michigan allows redemption between thirty and 365 days, depending on mortgage documents.
- Minnesota allows redemption between six and twelve months, depending on mortgage documents.
- North Dakota allows redemption between 100 and 365 days, depending on mortgage documents.
- Some states only allow redemption in cases that are handled as judicial foreclosures. These include Alaska, Arkansas, and California.
- New Mexico allows redemption between thirty and 270 days, depending on mortgage documents.
- Oregon and Vermont allow redemption in 180 days if the foreclosure was a judicial foreclosure.
- Some states give only ninety days for redemption. These are Illinois, Maine, and Wyoming.
- Colorado allows only seventy-five days for redemption.
- South Dakota allows sixty days for redemption if the property is abandoned; otherwise, it allows six months.
- Wisconsin allows sixty days for redemption if the property is abandoned; otherwise, it allows six to twelve months.
- Iowa allows twenty days for redemption.
- New Jersey allows ten days for redemption.
- Connecticut, Maryland, and Utah leave the question of whether or not to allow redemption to the court handling the judicial foreclosure.

Question 131. What is the process of appealing a foreclosure sale?

If the borrower finds errors in his notice of default or in any other document relating to the foreclosure sale, he may be able to appeal the sale. Foreclosure documents can contain errors such as misspelled names, erroneous legal descriptions, inaccurate street addresses, and mathematical errors in calculating the amount due for legal fees, interest, and late-payment charges. Any of the errors could make the process flawed and give the borrower the right to appeal.

The borrower also may notice that there were procedural errors during the service of documents or that the lender failed to adhere to statutory foreclosure sale procedures, which could result in a court's overturning a foreclosure sale. Any error entitles the borrower to file a case to redeem the auction sale. Even if you won the bid, you could lose the property if the borrower successfully redeems the sale.

Question 132. **How much cash will you need?**

The amount of cash you need at the auction depends on the rules in your state. Some states require all bidders to pay the amount bid in full with a cashier's check at the auction, others allow you to pay a certain percentage at the auction and then give you thirty to ninety days to come up with the rest. Before bidding at any foreclosure auction, be sure you know exactly how much cash you will need if you win a bid. Call your county sheriff's office and ask for the person who coordinates the auctions. He can give you a complete listing of the auction rules and processes, so you will be prepared on the day of the auction. You will lose the property if you can't meet the cash requirements the day of the auction.

Question 133. **How much competition can you expect?**

Like competition for any property, the amount of competition you can expect depends on the location of the property and its condition. If the property is in a bad part of town and looks in need of extensive repair even from outside the house, you likely will not find a lot of competition for that property at the auction. But if the property is in a good neighborhood and appears to be in good condition, expect there to be a competitive bidding process. If the property you want does end up in a competitive bidding process, don't get caught up in auction fever. Stick to the price you set prior to going to the auction.

Question 134. **What type of foreclosure expenses can you expect?**

Each state sets its own fees, but some of the fees you can expect to pay include a public-trustee release fee, recording fees, tax stamps, and foreclosure fees based on the purchase price. Most of the fees are similar to the state fees paid for any home purchase. These fees will be added to the foreclosure expenses already calculated into the amount due for the property. Legal fees, foreclosure-filing fees, and other fees incurred by the lender will be covered in the sale price that you bid.

Question 135. **What are foreclosure costs, fees, and expenses?**

Your total costs, fees, and expenses will vary depending upon what you choose to do yourself and what services you hire out to someone else. You could incur expenses from your attorney or title company to research any legal ownership issues, liens, and mortgages. You could incur expenses if you choose to hire an appraiser to get an estimate of the property's value.

Each state has its own set of fees for closing on a property after foreclosure. Check with your county sheriff for complete details on the fees you may expect if you purchase a foreclosure property.

Question 136. **What is the value of an appraiser when buying a foreclosure property?**

If you think you have a good handle on property values in the area where you plan to buy foreclosure properties, you don't have to hire an appraiser. But if you are not sure you know current property values, an appraiser can save you a huge loss and help you to avoid properties whose loan balance is actually higher than the current market value of the home.

In a weak real estate market where prices are falling, it is not unusual for a property to be financed for more than it is currently worth. Also, some lenders allow people to borrow up to 125 percent of the home's value, so the mortgage due totals considerably more than the home is worth.

Don't automatically assume a property is worth the amount the lender seeks. By the time all the legal costs, past-due payments, interest, foreclosure fees, and other administrative fees are added to a loan balance, the amount due can be dramatically more than the market value. Do your homework, and if you have any doubts about the market value, hire an appraiser before you bid on the house.

Chapter **8**

AFTER A FORECLOSURE SALE

If the lender is stuck with the property after a foreclosure sale, it will want to sell the property as quickly as possible. This is when you might be able to get your best deal. These properties are called real estate owned, or REOs for short. This chapter covers REOs and how you can buy them.

Question 137. What happens if a property does not sell at an auction?

When a property does not sell at auction, the lender that initiated the foreclosure gets the property. It must then figure out the quickest way to sell the property. Most lenders have REO departments, whose job it is to find the best deal in the shortest possible time. If a property that you are interested in during the pre-foreclosure period ends up as a REO property, you can probably buy it for less than the total amount due on the loan balance.

Question 138. **Can you buy property after a foreclosure sale?**

Sometimes you may be able to work out a short-sale (as discussed in Chapter 6) on the day of the foreclosure. While you might have had difficulty getting the homeowner to agree to a short-sale or getting the loss-mitigation department to accept your offer, the lender might be much more willing to negotiate if it was unable to find a better deal at auction. If the lender still isn't ready, you may be able to work out the deal you want with the REO department.

Question 139. **What is real-estate-owned (REO) property?**

Real-estate-owned (REO) properties are properties in a lender's portfolio that have been taken over by the lender after a foreclosure. You can get some great deals buying REO properties. You will even be able to inspect the property prior to an offer, but you will have to buy the property "as is," which means you can't expect the bank to come up with any money to repair any problems you see.

Question 140. **How do you find out about REO property owned by a bank?**

The best way to find REO properties is to make contact with lenders that you know make mortgage loans and that you've seen listed in recent foreclosure auctions. Call and ask for their REO departments.

You will be able to find out what properties are currently in their REO portfolio. Look at the properties to determine if you want to make an offer on any of them. Once you've negotiated your first deal, you'll be considered a good source for future deals. The person you worked with may even start to call you if he thinks the lender has a property that might interest you.

Question 141. **How do you find out about REO property if owned by a private lender?**

REOs owned by private lenders or investors are often sold through a listing broker or asset-management company. If you are interested in a particular property that was taken over by a private investor at auction, contact the lender and find out who handles the sale of REO properties.

Also, talk with brokers in your area to find out who deals in REO properties. If you build a strong working relationship with an REO listing broker, you will be contacted when a good deal becomes available.

Question 142. **How do you find VA REOs?**

If a home that interests you was financed through the U.S. Department of Veterans Affairs and was taken over by the VA as the result of a foreclosure, you will find that listing through its contracted property management service, Ocwen Loan Servicing, LLC, which is located in West Palm Beach, Florida.

You can get a list of properties for sale on Ocwen's Web site, at *www.ocwen.com*. If a property interests you, you must contact a local real estate broker to see the property and arrange for a purchase. All VA properties are listed with local listing agents through the local multiple listing systems (MLS).

Question 143. **What terms will the lender offer you on financing the property?**

You can get the best terms on a REO deal if you are ready to put cash on the table. Prequalifying for financing before you even start talking about a deal will put you in a strong bargaining position.

Some lenders will allow you to cure an existing loan, which means to pay all past-due amounts and foreclosure fees and then take over the payments on the loan. Whether or not that is a good deal depends upon how many months have gone by since the original borrower stopped making payments.

Question 144. **How much cash will you need?**

The amount of actual cash you will need depends upon the type of financing you can arrange for the property. If you are planning to take over the original loan, the amount needed will be the amount necessary to cure the loan. Often to get rid of the property a lender will likely be willing to settle for less than the amount necessary to cure the loan.

Obviously, you should try to get the property with the least cash possible so you will have the money you need to fix up the property and put it on the market. Fixing up and flipping foreclosure purchases is covered in Chapter 13.

Question 145. **What type of qualification process will you need to go through?**

If you want to take over an existing mortgage, expect the lender to be very strict about documentation of your income and ability to pay the loan. The lender definitely will not want to risk another foreclosure on that property. You may be able to get a great deal from the lender if the lender sees you as a safe bet to turn a nonperforming property (an REO) into one that goes back to the income-producing category.

Once you've bought and sold a few foreclosure properties, you should have a good working relationship with several lenders. After they get to know you and know that you handle the deals professionally, you will find it easier to get approval for financing. Chapter 11 covers funding a foreclosure purchase.

Chapter **9**

BANKRUPTCIES AND THE FORECLOSURE PROCESS

A homeowner can stop a foreclosure by filing for a bankruptcy. If you find out that a homeowner is planning to file for a bankruptcy, walk away from the property for the time being. This chapter explains the bankruptcy process and how it can affect foreclosures.

Question 146. **What is a bankruptcy?**

Bankruptcy is a legal process that allows debtors to get a fresh financial start by wiping out all their debt. Anyone has the right to file for bankruptcy by federal law, and all bankruptcy cases are handled in a federal court.

When a debtor files for bankruptcy, he immediately stops all calls from creditors who are trying to collect their money. The court decides who gets paid and how much they will be paid.

The bankruptcy can eliminate the legal obligation to pay most of a debtor's unsecured debts, but it can't stop debtors from losing their homes unless they are able to repay that debt. In some cases, a person is able to cure (bring up to date) a mortgage after a bankruptcy, in which the debtor gets rid of the burden of unsecured debt. In other cases, debtors find out they still must sell their homes to avoid foreclosure.

Question 147. **Can an owner stop a foreclosure through bankruptcy?**

When a bankruptcy is filed, the court takes control of the debtor's financial life. All creditors must work through the bankruptcy trustee to collect their money. They can no longer contact the debtor directly. Since a bankruptcy takes at least three to four months (and often longer, depending upon how backed up the court is), this does give the debtor some time to get his financial ducks in order without being hounded by creditors.

When a debtor files for bankruptcy, he can stop all foreclosures, repossessions, and wage garnishments through a special court order of protection, which is executed the day bankruptcy is filed. This is called an automatic stay (discussed in question 152).

Question 148. **What is a Chapter 7 bankruptcy?**

When a debtor files for a Chapter 7 bankruptcy, he asks the bankruptcy court to discharge all of his debts, which means any unsecured credit will be wiped out to zero dollars. But if the debtor has secured debts, such as the mortgage on his home or loan on his car, he will have to give up property to discharge that debt.

If you are interested in a property and the homeowner tells you he's planning to file for bankruptcy, don't try to arrange a pre-foreclosure sale. The homeowner isn't ready to talk. He may be ready when he finds out that he can't come up with the cash to save his home from foreclosure. Stay in touch with the homeowner, and let him know you are interested if he does decide to sell in the future.

Question 149. **What is a Chapter 11 bankruptcy?**

A Chapter 11 bankruptcy is one used primarily by businesses so they can stop their creditors from collecting and have time to reorganize their debts. Individuals who consider Chapter 11 bankruptcy have assets above one or both of the Chapter 13 bankruptcy limits. Their unsecured debts exceed $307,675 or their secured debts exceed $922,975 or both are true.

It's much more expensive to file for a Chapter 11 bankruptcy: $839. To file for Chapter 7, current court costs are $209. Lawyers fees are on top of that, but those vary greatly. In addition, there are fees that must be paid quarterly throughout the time the court is managing the debtor's debt payment. For example, if the disbursements total less than $15,000, the quarterly fee would be at least $250 and could go as high as $10,000 per quarter if disbursements were to exceed $5 million.

Question 150. **What is a Chapter 13 bankruptcy?**

When a debtor files a Chapter 13 bankruptcy, he must show how he will pay off some of his past-due and current debts over three to five years. He is allowed to keep his home and car, provided that he can make the regular monthly payments on the mortgage and car loan with some extra payments to get caught up on the amount that is past due.

A Chapter 13 bankruptcy can help the debtor save his property. The bankruptcy court sets a monthly payment that the debtor must make to the trustee and that the trustee then pays out to the creditors.

Question 151. **What is a bankruptcy trustee?**

The bankruptcy court excises control over the debtor's financial affairs through the appointment of a person called the bankruptcy trustee. The trustee handles the case on behalf of the bankruptcy court and seeks to ensure that unsecured creditors are paid as much as possible on the debts that are owed them. He also makes sure that the debtor complies with the bankruptcy laws.

The trustee can be a local bankruptcy attorney or someone else knowledgeable about Chapter 7 or Chapter 13 bankruptcy procedures, in addition to the court's operations, rules, and procedures. If the trustee is not an attorney, he may be a businessperson who is knowledgeable about finances and personal bankruptcy.

Question 152. **What is an automatic stay?**

An automatic stay goes into effect immediately after the debtor files for bankruptcy. This stay prohibits creditors and collection agencies from taking any action to collect the money owed to them. The automatic stay stops all bills, lawsuits, repossessions, foreclosures, and IRS liens.

Sometimes a creditor will file a motion to lift the stay. Others may begin collection proceedings without seeking permission from the court. Under the new bankruptcy law, the court is more likely to give them permission to continue trying to collect, but for most types of debt, creditors are stopped in their tracks from making harassing calls to collect debt, sending threatening attorney's letters, or filing a lawsuit seeking a monetary judgment. Domestic-relations proceedings, evictions (obtained prior to bankruptcy filing), and many tax proceedings are not stopped by the automatic stay.

Question 153. **How can owners use the stay process to avoid foreclosure?**

A stay will stop a lender from foreclosing on the property, but a lender can file to lift the stay. If the debtor is not able to cure the loan (pay the total amount in arrears, plus any fees and legal costs) or work out a payment arrangement that includes making payments toward past-due amounts, the court could lift the stay. Foreclosures on a home cannot be stopped if the debtor filed for another bankruptcy in the previous two years and that court lifted the stay in that proceeding.

Chapter **10**

ESCROW AND CLOSING

Closing on a foreclosure property can be filled with surprises. Hopefully you've done your homework well and have unearthed most of the potential pitfalls. This chapter reviews the escrow and closing process for foreclosure properties.

Question 154. **What is escrow?**

Escrow is a means of transferring or exchanging property that you own through the services of a neutral third party. In most states, escrow agents are professionals who have been trained and accredited to handle this transfer or exchange.

During the escrow process, the buyer of the property transfers funds or has the bank transfer funds to the escrow agent. The seller of the property transfers the property ownership to the escrow property. When all contract provisions are met, the escrow agent then assigns the property to the buyer and disburses the money to pay off any debts or liens and gives any remaining money to the seller.

Question 155. **How do you pick an escrow holder?**

Most title companies can serve as escrow holders and often the real estate agent, if a real estate is involved, will recommend the escrow agent. The agent can be any qualified professional whom both parties—buyer and seller—agree to use.

An escrow agent is primarily concerned about the proper completion of the paperwork and the disbursal of the funds. He is not allowed to provide legal, accounting, or financial advice. He cannot act as a mediator or negotiator if a surprise pops up at closing—such as a lien that was not discovered prior to the contract.

You have the right to pick your own escrow agent. You should close any deal on foreclosure property using a real estate attorney well versed in handling foreclosure properties. He will protect your interests and be sure that you are getting a clean title. If a surprise comes up at closing, he can assist in negotiating a solution to the problem and continue the closing.

Question 156. **What are escrow instructions?**

Escrow instructions are developed based on the parties involved in the transactions. Most of these instructions are based on provisions in the contract to purchase the property, and the remainder is written by the lender who will be financing the property.

The escrow agent closes the real estate transaction based on these escrow transactions. Once all conditions that are stated in the instructions have been met, the escrow can be closed, the money can be disbursed, and the title can be transferred.

Question 157. **What is an escrow closing?**

The actual escrow closing takes place when the buyer and seller complete all the documentation is front of the neutral third party and meet all the conditions laid out in the escrow instructions.

Sometimes a lender will require you to bring certain documentation to closing and will not allow you to close until that documentation is submitted. Other times you might actually sign your loan application at closing because you made arrangements for the loan by telephone. If the instructions from the lender require certain actions, the escrow agent is the one to be sure those actions have been completed before he can disburse the funds.

The actual duties of the escrow agent at closing are to follow any instructions given by the parties—buyer, seller, lender, and borrower—and to handle the transaction in a timely manner. This includes handling all funds, paying all bills as authorized, responding to any questions that arise (but not offering legal, financial, or accounting advice), and preparing an accounting of the funds disbursed. The accounting is done on the HUD 1 Settlement Statement.

Question 158. **What is a quick-cash system?**

One quick way to make money buying and selling foreclosure properties is to use a quick-cash system. In this system, you find a third party who is interested in the investment property.

After you've got a deal in place, you find an investor interested in the property who does not want to do all the legwork of finding and negotiating foreclosure deals. You assign the contract to this third party for a fee. At closing, you get the fee, and the investor takes control of the property and puts up the cash.

Question 159. **What is a closing statement?**

The closing statement is an accounting of all funds disbursed as part of the closing. Any time you've closed on a real estate property, the closing statement, known as a HUD 1 Settlement Statement (a form designed by the U.S. Department of Housing and Urban Development), will detail where all the money went. It includes an extensive list of all possible costs that must be paid by both the buyer and seller. It also includes the details of how those funds are disbursed, which can be for taxes, to pay off existing liens, payment of all mortgage holders, and payment of anything else designated in the closing instructions.

Question 160. **What is title insurance?**

Title insurance protects you from any future claims that might be made on the property. If someone tries to claim ownership of the property or seeks payment for an unpaid lien, the title insurer will be responsible for fighting that battle for you and paying any money that may be owed.

Question 161. **What is a title search?**

A title search is a thorough review of all information filed against a piece of property. This will include any mortgages, liens, judgments, and claims of ownership. You should never close on a property, foreclosure or not, without first paying for a title search. While title searches do occasionally miss a hidden lien, that is a very rare occasion. You will not be able to get title insurance unless you pay for a title search.

Question 162. **What is an owner's policy?**

The owner's title insurance policy protects an owner if a claim is made against the property after the sale of the property. If the claim results in monetary damages, the title insurance company will pay the claim and protect your interests.

You should get an owner's policy whenever you are selling property that you bought pre- or post-foreclosure. You likely don't know the full history of the property, and you need to protect yourself against claims that could be made that were not found during a title search.

Question 163. **What is a buyer's policy?**

A buyer's policy protects the person who bought real estate from a possible loss due to claims against that property. As the buyer, you are protected against any claims on the property that were not found in the public records. While a policy bought for a lender will cover any claims up to the value of the mortgage, only a buyer's policy issued by a title insurance company will protect the buyer's interests above the value of the mortgage.

Question 164. **What is a lender's policy?**

Any time you buy property with a mortgage, the lender will require you to buy a lender's policy. This policy issued by a title insurance company will protect the interests of the lender. If a claim that was missed as part of the title search is brought against the property after the closing, the title insurance company will have to pay any monetary damages.

Question 165. **Why should you use a real estate attorney?**

You should always use a real estate attorney when closing on a foreclosure property. Only a real estate attorney will represent you and your interests. The escrow agent must remain neutral and cannot give any legal advice.

You should be sure your real estate attorney can bring the following key knowledge to the closing table:

- Working knowledge of real property statutory regulations and any case law that has arisen from those regulations
- Experience in solving complex legal problems involving real estate transactions
- Understanding of liens, judgment liens, and foreclosure actions

Only an attorney that you hire has a fiduciary obligation to act in your best interests.

Question 166. **What is the Real Estate Settlement Procedures Act?**

The 1974 Real Estate Settlement Procedures Act (RESPA) protects consumers from kickbacks or referral fees that can increase settlement costs. In fact, a lot of that extra paperwork you sign at closing relates to requirements of RESPA.

RESPA is the law that requires you, as a borrower, to receive disclosures about loan costs associated with settlement, lender services, and escrow account practices, as well as details about the relationship between the lender and the settlement agent. Referral fees are specifically prohibited for settlement service business when a federal mortgage loan is involved. You also cannot be required to purchase title insurance based on RESPA regulations. For more information on RESPA, go to *www.hud.gov/offices/hsg/sfh/res/respa_hm.cfm.*

Chapter **11**

FUNDING A FORECLOSURE PURCHASE

While you may hear lots of promotions for systems of buying fore-closure property with no cash down, you will probably find that to purchase decent property, you need some cash up front. There are many different ways you can come up with the cash you need to buy a foreclosure property. This chapter covers some of your key options.

Question 167. How do you fund the purchase of a fore-closure property?

There are essentially three types of residential real estate loans: the conventional loan, FHA mortgage, and VA mortgage. Private mortgages can also be found. (Chapter 1 discusses the types of mortgages.)

If you are buying and selling foreclosure properties, you will be seen as an investor. You will find that loans written to conform with the rules of the two key mortgage funders—Fannie Mae (Federal National Mortgage Association) and Freddie Mac (Federal Home Loan Mortgage Corporation)—set limits on investors. You cannot have more than ten loans on one-to-four-unit residential properties at one time. This does include your residence as well as your investment properties.

You need start-up capital to get your foreclosure business off the ground. You can do that using unsecured credit, home equity lines, borrowing from family and friends, or borrowing from the equity of a life insurance policy.

Question 168. **How can I borrow against a life insurance policy?**

If you have a life insurance policy that has a cash value (a whole life policy), you may be able to get some quick cash at a very low interest rate. You can call the customer service number for your insurance company and find out your maximum allowable loan on the policy, as well as the interest rate you must pay.

The major risk you take when you borrow from an insurance policy is that the outstanding balance of the loan will be subtracted from the face value of the life insurance policy if you should die prior to paying back the loan. Your beneficiaries would get less money than you planned for them to receive.

Question 169. **How can I use small amounts of money from different banks?**

As long as you have a good credit rating, you should be able to get cash using unsecured personal credit loans from two or three banks. Check with a number of banks to find out their loan rates, and choose two or three banks that offer you the best rates. You probably will get better rates from banks at which you already have accounts.

Question 170. **How can I use a home improvement line of credit?**

If you recently paid off the balance on a home improvement line of credit on your own property, you may be able to use those funds again toward fixing up the foreclosure property you buy. An equity line you already have in place will give you the quick cash that you need to fix up the property and flip it. You can then quickly repay the home improvement loan and have it available to use on the next property you choose.

Question 171. **How can I use an equity loan?**

If you have a home equity loan in place, that can be a very fast way to get some quick cash to close on a pre-foreclosure property. If you've worked out a good deal with a lender in which you plan to reinstate the loan on the property of someone nearing foreclosure by curing the loan (paying all monies due to get the loan current), you can use the equity loan on your residence to come up with the cash you need.

That way you quickly get the cash you need to close within thirty days, and you have a loan in place to cover the costs of buying the foreclosure. After fixing up the property, you can sell it, pay off the original mortgage, and use your profits to pay off the money you took from your equity loan. Hopefully you've made enough profits to have the cash for your next foreclosure property—or you can always draw from your equity loan again.

Question 172. **How can I use a line of credit?**

If you don't want to put your own home at risk and you have a good relationship with a bank, you may be able to set up a line of credit for your foreclosure business. You can draw cash when needed to buy and repay the line of credit when you flip the property. As long as you have a history of using credit responsibly, you shouldn't have difficulty arranging a line of credit.

Question 173. **How can I use a VA loan?**

If you find a foreclosure property with a loan secured by the VA, you may be able to save a lot of cash up front. The U.S. Department of Veterans Affairs must refund any losses by the lender in the event of a foreclosure. To minimize the loss, the VA will pay up to 6 percent of the value of the purchase toward closing costs. You can even get the property without a down payment. Discounts on these homes range from 10 to 50 percent of market value. If you are not a veteran, you can still take advantage of these benefits and get financing for the loan. The VA will not make any repairs. You will have to buy the home in as-is condition, which is true for all property after foreclosure. See question 142 for more information on how to find VA foreclosure properties.

Question 174. **How do I find a partner with cash?**

If you don't want to borrow money to start buying foreclosures, your only other option is to find a partner who has the cash. An interested family or friend would be a good option, but if you don't know anyone, you would then need to find such a partner by talking with others who buy and sell foreclosures in your area.

Some people have the cash, but they don't have the time to do all the legwork and research it takes to line up foreclosure deals. You may first work with a good potential partner by using the quick-cash system mentioned in question 158 to flip properties you found by assigning a foreclosure contract to him for a fee. After doing a few deals that way, you may be able to negotiate a more significant cut by forming a partnership. If you do decide to partner with someone, be sure to work with an attorney to draft a partnership agreement that protects your interest in the business.

Question 175. **What is a hard-money lender?**

A hard-money lender is an investor who loans money for real estate purchases privately without requiring the strict underwriting guidelines that most financial institutions require. There are two big advantages of working with a hard-money lender: It will take less time to get the money, and you can qualify for the loan more easily. You will pay higher interest rates to hard-money lenders, so only choose this route if you can't get better interest rates elsewhere.

Question 176. **How can I work with a bank or other lending institution?**

If the lending institution has already started the foreclosure process on a property, you will find a favorable ear if you are willing to cure the loan (pay cash to bring the loan current) and make a nonperforming property (one that is not earning anything for the lender) a performing property (where interest is being earned).

Lending institutions do not want to foreclose on properties and take possession. They prefer to get rid of foreclosure properties as quickly as possible. If you can show the lending institution that you are creditworthy and can come up with the cash, you should be able to get some excellent terms to take over a problem property and reinstate the loan.

Question 177. **How can I find lenders who will finance a foreclosure?**

You should start with the lender who holds the mortgage on the property. Often, you won't need to even apply for a new loan; instead, you will just have to come up with the cash needed to reinstate the existing loan and take it over.

If the foreclosure is already complete and the property is a REO property (as discussed in Chapter 8), you may even be able to avoid paying at least part of the past-due payments and foreclosure costs. Once a lender owns properties, it wants to get rid of them as quickly as possible. The lender has already discovered at auction (where there were no bidders) that it can't get the full amount it wants on the property.

Question 178. **When should I apply for financing?**

You should apply for financing before you make an offer to buy a foreclosure property. You will need to show that you can come up with the cash at closing. Being able to show to a lender that you are already prequalified and that you have the cash in hand that is needed to close will make it much easier for you to negotiate with the lender that holds the mortgage on the property.

Question 179. **What is "subject to" existing financing?**

When you buy a property subject to existing financing, it means that you take title to the property subject to the existing mortgage or deed-of-trust loan. This is very risky business, and in most cases you will be in violation of the due-on-sale clause of the contract. If the lender finds out, he has the right to call the loan and require you to pay the mortgage in full immediately. If you can't come up with the cash, the lender has the right to foreclose on the property.

You may be able to work with the lender and take over the mortgage legitimately, but your best bet is not to even try. You should be able to work out a deal with a lender once the foreclosure process is started.

Question 180. **How can I take over "subject to" financing?**

You shouldn't even try to take title to a property subject to existing financing. The only exception is if, after carefully reading the mortgage or deed of trust, you find out that there is no due-on-sale clause, which is almost unheard of in today's world. If the homeowner resists allowing you to work a deal directly with the lender, walk away from the property and save yourself a lot of problems.

Chapter **12**

DISCOVERING STATE-BY-STATE FORECLOSURE AND HOMESTEAD EXEMPTION RULES

Each state enacts its own laws regarding how the foreclosure of a home should be carried out. By being aware of the foreclosure laws, you can discuss the process with homeowners you approach to buy a foreclosure, as well as use the information to find homes nearing foreclosure.

A borrower can stop a foreclosure at least temporarily by filing for bankruptcy. A bankruptcy can't discharge a secured lien, such as a mortgage, but it may be able to give the borrower time to bring his mortgage current and keep his home.

This chapter also covers homestead exemptions, which give the borrower additional protection to help him save his home if he files for bankruptcy. You should know the homestead exemptions for the states in which you buy foreclosure properties. In most states, once you find out the borrower is filing for bankruptcy, your best bet is to walk away. Still, you should keep your eye on the process in case the homeowner is not able to save his home with the bankruptcy.

Question 181. **What are the foreclosure and homestead exemption rules specific to Alabama?**

Alabama lenders can foreclose on a property using either a judicial foreclosure or a nonjudicial foreclosure. The nonjudicial foreclosure is used when a power-of-sale clause exists in the deed of trust.

In some deeds of trust, the power-of-sale clause will specify the time, place, and terms of a sale. If that is the case in your deed of trust, that specified procedure must be followed. If not, the foreclosure sale takes place at the front or main door of the county courthouse where the property is located after a default of the deed of trust or mortgage. The sale may take place thirty days after the last notice of sale is published, and the property will be sold for cash to the highest bidder. Notice of sale must be published once a week for four successive weeks in a newspaper published in the county or counties where the property is located. The notice of sale must give the time, place, and terms of sale along with a description of the property. If no power of sale is contained in a mortgage or deed of trust, then the lender must file a lawsuit to foreclose after the mortgage or deed of trust is in default. Take advantage of this publishing detail to find foreclosure properties you may want to consider.

Alabama does allow homeowners to redeem their property for twelve months after the foreclosure sale. If the homeowner decides to file for bankruptcy to stop the foreclosure, his homestead exemption is $5,000, and the property in question cannot exceed 160 acres. If there is more equity than that in the property, the bankruptcy trustee could force the sale of the property.

Question 182. **What are the foreclosure and homestead exemption rules specific to Alaska?**

Lenders in Alaska can foreclose on property using a judicial or nonjudicial foreclosure. If a judicial foreclosure is used, the process is carried out according to the rules of equity. Deficiency suits are permitted, and the borrower will not have a right of redemption.

If a power-of-sale clause exists in the mortgage or deed of trust, the nonjudicial foreclosure process will be used. If the power-of-sale clause specified time, place, and terms of sale, that procedure is followed as long as it meets the minimum protections specified under Alaska state law. Here are the steps a lender must take to successfully complete a nonjudicial foreclosure in Alaska:

- Trustee must record a notice of default in the office of the recorder in the district where the property is located not less than thirty days after default and not less than three months before the sale.
- The notice of default must include the name of the borrower, as well as the book and page where the deed is recorded. It also must describe the property and details about the borrower's default, the amount the borrower owes, and the fact that the trustee wants to sell the property. Finally, it must include the date, time, and place of sale.
- Within ten days of recording the notice of default, the trustee must send a copy by certified mail to the last known address of the borrower, the current occupant, and any other individuals or companies that have a claim or lien on the property.
- The borrower must be permitted to cure the default and stop the foreclosure by paying all past-due amounts plus attorney's fees. The lender cannot require that the borrower repay the entire remaining principal balance to cure the default.
- The sale of the property must take place at a public auction held at the front door of a courthouse of the superior court

in the judicial district where the property is located. The trustee must sell the property to the highest bidder, which can be the lender.

If the borrower decides to file for bankruptcy to stop a fore-closure, the homestead exemption for Alaska residents is $67,500.

Question 183. **What are the foreclosure and homestead exemption rules specific to Arizona?**

Lenders in Arizona can use a judicial or nonjudicial foreclosure process. The judicial foreclosure process is used when there is no power-of-sale clause in the mortgage or deed of trust.

For a nonjudicial foreclosure, if the power-of-sale clause specifies the time, place, and terms of sale, then those procedures are followed. If not, here are the procedures for carrying out a nonjudicial foreclosure sale:

- The trustee must record the notice of sale at the county recorder's office in the county in which the property is located. Within five days of recording the notice, the trustee must send by certified mail a copy of the notice to any person named in the trust deed. He also must publish a notice in a newspaper in the county where the property is located once a week for four consecutive weeks. The last notice must be published not less than ten days prior to the sale.
- The trustee or his agent must conduct the sale, which must be for cash to the highest bidder. If the lender is the highest bidder, he can make a credit bid, which means he will cancel out all or part of the money the borrower owed the lender rather than pay cash.
- The successful high bidder must pay the bid price by 5 p.m. the next business day after the bid. If the high bidder doesn't pay, the trustee may postpone the sale to another time and place. The successful bidder gets a trustee's deed.

- After the sale is completed, the proceeds go to pay the obligations secured by the deed of trust that was foreclosed, and then the junior lien holders are paid.
- If the amount paid at auction is less than the amount due, the lender cannot bring a deficiency suit against the person who lost the property if it is 2.5 acres or less and was a single-family or two-family dwelling. A deficiency suit is allowed on other types of property as long as it is filed within ninety days.

If the borrower decides to file for bankruptcy to stop the foreclosure, the maximum Arizona homestead exemption is $150,000.

Question 184. **What are the foreclosure and homestead exemption rules specific to Arkansas?**

Arkansas lenders can foreclose on deeds of trust or mortgages using a judicial or nonjudicial foreclosure process. Lenders must do an appraisal of the property before scheduling the date of foreclosure.

If a property is offered for sale and does not get an offer for two-thirds of the appraised value or more, the property must be offered for sale again in twelve months. At a second sale, the highest bidder gets the property without consideration of an appraisal.

If a judicial foreclosure is used, the court will decree the amount of the borrower's debt and give him a short time to pay that debt. If he doesn't pay in that time, the clerk of the court advertises the property for sale. The lender may bid by crediting a portion (or all) of the amount the court found due to the lender against the sale price of the property. If the property does not sell for an amount equal to what is due, the lender may seize other property from the borrower. The borrower has one year from the date of sale to redeem the property by paying the amount at which the property was sold plus interest.

If a power-of-sale clause exists in the mortgage or deed to trust, then a nonjudicial foreclosure can be used. Here is the process for non-foreclosure sales:

- The trustee must record the notice of sale in the county recorder's office of the county where the property is located. The notice of default and intention to sell must be mailed by certified mail to the borrower within thirty days of the recording. Within five days after the notice is recorded, the trustee must send by certified mail a copy of the notice of sale to all parties to the trust deed. In addition, the notice of default and intention to sell must appear in a county newspaper where the property is located once a week for four consecutive weeks, with the last notice being published not less than ten days prior to the date of sale.
- Any person, including the lender, may bid at the sale. The high bidder must pay the bid at the time of the sale or within ten days. The lender may bid by canceling out what is owed on the loan, including unpaid taxes, insurance, costs of sale, and maintenance.
- After the completion of the sale, the proceeds go toward paying the expenses of the foreclosure sale and then toward the obligations of the secured trust deed that was foreclosed. After that, junior lien holders are paid. The original borrower is entitled to get any remaining funds. The successful bidder gets a trustee's deed.

The lender may sue the borrower for any deficiency of funds within twelve months of the power-of-sale foreclosure. The lender can sue for the difference between the foreclosure price and the balance due on the loan or the balance due on the loan minus the fair market value of the property, whichever is less.

If the borrower decides to file for bankruptcy to stop foreclosure, Arkansas offers a homestead exemption based on lot size. As long as the residence is on less than .25 acre in a city, town, or village, or less than 80 acres elsewhere in the state, it is protected by the homestead exemption rules. If the property is between .25 and 1.0 acre in a city, town, or village, or 80 to 160 acres elsewhere, an additional limit of $2,500 is provided. Homestead may not include property that is more than 1 acre in a city, town, or village or 160 acres elsewhere.

Question 185. **What are the foreclosure and homestead exemption rules specific to California?**

California lenders can foreclose on deeds of trusts or mortgages using either a judicial or nonjudicial foreclosure process. If there is no power-of-sale clause, a judicial process is used. After the court orders a foreclosure, the property is auctioned to the highest bidder. Lenders can seek a deficiency judgment, and sometimes the court will allow the borrower up to one year to redeem the property.

If there is a power-of-sale clause in the mortgage or deed of trust, the nonjudicial foreclosure process will be used. This includes the following:

- The lender must record a notice of sale in the county where the property is located at least fourteen days prior to the sale and send this notice by certified mail, with return receipt requested, to the borrower at least twenty days before the sale. The lender must also post on the property itself at least twenty days before the sale, as well as post in at least one public place in the county where the property is to be sold. The notice of sale must contain the time and location of the sale, plus the property address, the trustee's name, address, and phone number, and a statement indicating that the property will be sold at auction.
- The borrower can cure the default up to five days before the foreclosure sale to stop the process.
- The sale can be held on any business day between 9:00 a.m. and 5:00 p.m. It must take place at the location specified in the notice of sale. The property is sold to the highest bidder, and the trustee may require proof of the bidder's ability to pay the full bid amount.

Lenders may not seek a deficiency judgment after a nonjudicial foreclosure sale, and the borrower has no rights of redemption.

If a borrower decides to file for bankruptcy to save his home, California has two different homestead exemption systems. One allows a homestead exemption if the borrower is single and not disabled. Families are allowed a homestead exemption if no other member of the household has a homestead. People over sixty-five years of age or are physically or mentally disabled can claim a homestead exemption of $150,000. Borrowers may file a homestead declaration to protect their property from the attachment of a judgment lien or protect the proceeds of a voluntary sale for six months. The second system allows up to an $18,675 homestead exemption on a residence. This is used by people who don't have much equity in their property but do have other assets they want to keep.

Question 186. What are the foreclosure and homestead exemption rules specific to Colorado?

Colorado lenders can foreclose on mortgages or deeds of trust in default using either a judicial or nonjudicial process. If a judicial process is used, the home will be auctioned off to the highest bidder if the court orders the foreclosure.

A nonjudicial foreclosure is used if a power-of-sale clause exists in the mortgage or deed of trust. Here is the process for a power-of-sale foreclosure:

- The lender, or more likely his attorney, begins the process by filing the required documents with the office of the public trustee of the county where the property is located. The public trustee then files a notice of election and demand with the county clerk and recorder of the county. After the notice is recorded, it must be published in a county newspaper where the property is located for a period of five consecutive weeks. In addition, the public trustee must mail the same information within ten days after the publication of the notice of election and demand for sale to the borrower and any owner or claimant of record at the address given in the recorded instrument. The public trustee must also mail within twenty-one days before the foreclosure sale a notice to the borrower that describes how to redeem the property.

- The borrower may stop the foreclosure process by filing an intent to cure with the public trustee's office at least fifteen days prior to the foreclosure sale. Then he must pay the necessary amount to bring the loan current by noon the day before the foreclosure sale is scheduled.

- The foreclosure sale must be scheduled between forty-five and sixty days of the recording of the election and demand for sale. The public trustee will likely hold the sale at any entrance to the courthouse, unless other provisions were made in the deed of trust. Lenders do have the option to file a suit for deficiency in Colorado. Borrowers have up to seventy-five days after the sale to redeem the property by paying the foreclosure sale amount, plus interest.

If the borrower chooses to file for bankruptcy in Colorado to stop a foreclosure, he can claim a homestead exemption of up to $45,000. A spouse or child of a deceased owner may claim the exemption.

Question 187. **What are the foreclosure and homestead exemption rules specific to Connecticut?**

Connecticut lenders must use a judicial foreclosure process to foreclose on a mortgage in default. The judicial foreclosure process is carried out by either a strict foreclosure or a decree of sale.

If a strict foreclosure is used, then no actual foreclosure sale is held. If the lender succeeds in getting a court order determining the borrower is in default on his mortgage, the title transfers to the lender immediately. The court can establish a time in which the borrower may redeem the property. If the borrower fails to do so, the title goes to the lender, and the borrower has no further claim to the property. The lender then has thirty days to record the certificate of foreclosure, which must contain a description of the property, the foreclosure proceedings, the mortgage, and the date the title transferred to the lender.

If the foreclosure is to be completed with a decree of sale, the court sets the time and manner of the sale and appoints a committee to sell the property. The court also appoints three appraisers to determine the value of the property. The borrower can stop the foreclosure any time before the sale by paying the balance due on the mortgage.

Lenders may sue to obtain a deficiency judgment in Connecticut.

If the borrower decides to file for bankruptcy to stop a foreclosure, Connecticut allows a homestead exemption of up to $75,000.

Question 188. **What are the foreclosure and homestead exemption rules specific to Delaware?**

In Delaware, lenders must use a judicial foreclosure process to foreclose on a mortgage in default. Several different types of processes are possible, but the one used the most often is that known as *scire facias*. With this process, the lender doesn't have to prove the borrower is in default on his mortgage; instead, the borrower must prove he isn't.

The suit to obtain a foreclosure order is filed by the lender, and the borrower must appear to prove his case within thirty days of being served a writ, at which time he must provide evidence regarding why the foreclosure should not take place. If the court is not satisfied with the borrower's explanation and evidence, it will authorize a foreclosure sale.

The foreclosure sale must be conducted by the sheriff and held either at the courthouse or at the property itself at least fourteen days after the notice of sale is posted on the property or other public places throughout the county in which the property is located. The borrower cannot redeem the property once the court has confirmed the sale.

Delaware offers no homestead exemption if the borrower decides to file for bankruptcy. The only thing that can protect a property, if the borrower files for bankruptcy, is if the property is held in tenancy by the entirety and only one spouse files for the bankruptcy.

Question 189. **What are the foreclosure and homestead exemption rules specific to Florida?**

Florida lenders must use a judicial foreclosure process to foreclose on a mortgage in default. If the foreclosure claim is tried, it is done without a jury. Any court order will specify how the foreclosure must take place.

Whatever the court orders—whether by legal advertisement, publication, or notice—it is the responsibility of the lender to be sure such actions are taken. After the sale takes place, the sale's terms must be confirmed by the court that ordered the sale. The borrower has the right to redeem the property by paying the amount of the purchase price prior to the time of the sale confirmation by the court.

Until the sale is confirmed by the court, the buyer of the property will hold a certificate of sale. After the court confirms the sale, the buyer can take title by filing a certificate of title.

Lenders may sue to obtain a deficiency judgment in Florida.

If the borrower chooses to file for bankruptcy to stop a foreclosure, Florida offers a homestead exemption of up to .5 acre in a municipality and 160 acres elsewhere in the state. A spouse or child of a deceased owner may claim the exemption. The borrower may file a homestead declaration. Property held as tenancy by the entirety may be exempt against debts owed by only one spouse.

Question 190. **What are the foreclosure and homestead exemption rules specific to Georgia?**

Lenders in Georgia can foreclose on mortgages or deeds of trust using either a judicial or nonjudicial foreclosure process. The judicial foreclosure process is used when a no-power-of-sale clause exists in the mortgage or deed of trust. Usually, if the court orders a foreclosure, the property is sold at auction to the highest bidder.

A nonjudicial foreclosure is used when a power-of-sale clause exists. The process for a nonjudicial foreclosure includes the following:

- Notice must be mailed by certified mail, return receipt requested, to the borrower no later than fifteen days prior to the date of the foreclosure sale to the address given to the lender by written notice from the borrower. The notice must be published in a county newspaper where the sale will be held once a week for four weeks preceding the sale.
- All foreclosure sales are held the first Tuesday of the month between 10:00 a.m. and 4:00 p.m. at the courthouse.

Lenders can seek a deficiency judgment in Georgia.

If the borrower decides to file for bankruptcy to stop the foreclosure, Georgia allows a homestead exemption of up to $10,000.

Question 191. **What are the foreclosure and homestead exemption rules specific to Hawaii?**

Lenders in Hawaii can use either a judicial or nonjudicial foreclosure process. The judicial process involves a lawsuit to obtain a court order to foreclose if there is no power-of-sale clause in the mortgage or deed of trust. If the court orders a foreclosure, the property will likely be sold at auction to the highest bidder.

If a power-of-sale clause does exist, then a nonjudicial foreclosure will be used. Here is the process for a nonjudicial foreclosure:

■ Lender files a notice of intent to foreclose, which must be published in a newspaper with general circulation in the county where the property is located once a week for three successive weeks. In addition, copies of the notice must be mailed or delivered to the mortgagor, the borrower, any prior or junior creditors, and the state director of taxation. Also, the notice must be posted on the premises not less than twenty-one days before the day of sale. Notice must include the date, time, and place of the public sale; the dates and times of the two open houses of the property or a statement that there will be no open houses; the money owed to the mortgagee under the mortgage agreement; description of the mortgaged property, including the address or description of the location and the tax map key number of the property; the name of the mortgagor and the borrower; the name of the lender; the name of any prior or junior creditors that have a recorded lien on the property before a notice of default was recorded; the name, address, and telephone number of the person conducting the public sale; and the terms and conditions of the public sale.

■ The borrower may cure the default up to three days before the sale and stop the foreclosure by paying the lien debt, as well as any costs and reasonable attorney's fees, unless another agreement is made between the lender and the borrower.

■ The sale can be held no earlier than fourteen days after the last ad is published. The property is sold at auction to the highest bidder.

Hawaii offers no rights of redemption to the borrower.

If the borrower decides to file for bankruptcy to stop a foreclosure, Hawaii offers a head-of-family over age sixty-five a $30,000 homestead exemption. All others can get up to a $20,000 homestead exemption. Property held as tenancy by the entirety may be exempt against debts owed by only one spouse.

Question 192. **What are the foreclosure and homestead exemption rules specific to Idaho?**

Idaho lenders can foreclose on deeds of trust in default using a nonjudicial foreclosure process. Here is how the process works in Idaho:

- A notice of sale must be recorded in the county where the property is located and given to the borrower and the occupants of the property (if not the borrower) at least 120 days before the date of the sale. In addition, the notice must be published in the county newspapers where the property is located at least once a week for four consecutive weeks. The final ad must be run at least thirty days before the foreclosure. The published notice must include a legal description of the property, its street address, and the name and phone number of someone who can give directions to the property. The notice also must include the nature of the default, a legal description of the property, as well as its street address, the lender's name, the date, time, and place of the sale, and the name and phone number of the person conducting the sale.
- The foreclosure sale must take place at the date, time, and place specified in the notice, but the sale may be postponed and held at a new time and place within thirty days of the originally scheduled sale.

The borrower can redeem the property during a six-month period if the property is less than twenty acres in size. If the property comprises more than twenty acres, the borrower has one year to redeem the property.

If the borrower decides to file for bankruptcy to stop the foreclosure, Idaho allows a homestead exemption up to $50,000. You must record a homestead exemption for property that is not yet occupied.

Question 193. **What are the foreclosure and homestead exemption rules specific to Illinois?**

Lenders in Illinois have three different options to foreclose on a mortgage in default: a judicial foreclosure, a deed in lieu of foreclosure, and a consent foreclosure. Here are how the three options work:

- If a judicial foreclosure is used, the lender must give the borrower a notice of intent to foreclose at least thirty days prior to the court's foreclosure judgment. If the court finds in favor of the lender and issues a notice of sale, the sale must be conducted based on the terms and conditions specified by the court. The sheriff or any judge within the county where the property is located may conduct the sale. The borrower has no rights of redemption after the foreclosure sale.
- If the borrower and lender reach agreement for a deed in lieu of foreclosure, the borrower may give the deed to the lender, and his interests in the property are terminated. If the lender agrees and accepts the deed, it can't seek to obtain a deficiency judgment against the borrower.
- If the court orders a consent foreclosure to satisfy the mortgage by giving title to the property to the lender, the borrower has no right of redemption. The lender also may not file for a deficiency judgment.

If the borrower decides to file for bankruptcy to stop foreclosure, Illinois offers a $7,500 homestead exemption. A spouse or child can claim the homestead exemption of a deceased owner. Illinois does recognize tenancy by the entirety with some limitations.

Question 194. **What are the foreclosure and homestead exemption rules specific to Indiana?**

Indiana lenders must use the judicial foreclosure process to close on a mortgage in default. Usually, after the court orders a foreclosure, the property is auctioned to the highest bidder.

In Indiana, there is a waiting time between the date the suit is filed and the day the property is sold. The date the mortgage was signed determines the length of time a lender must wait between filing the suit and proceeding with the foreclosure sale and can vary from three to twelve months. The owner may file a waiver of the time limit, which allows the sale to proceed without delay. If the borrower waives the wait time, the lender can file for a deficiency judgment.

If a foreclosure sale is ordered by the court, the lender must publish an ad once a week for three weeks. The first ad must be run thirty days before the sale. At the time the first ad is run, each owner must be served with notice of the foreclosure sale by the sheriff. The sheriff conveys title by a deed given immediately after the sale. The owner may reside in the property, rent free, until the foreclosure sale, provided the owner is not destroying the property.

If the borrower chooses to file for bankruptcy to stop a foreclosure, Indiana provides a homestead exemption of $7,500.

Question 195. **What are the foreclosure and homestead exemption rules specific to Iowa?**

Iowa lenders can foreclose on a mortgage in default using either a judicial or alternative nonjudicial foreclosure process. For a judicial foreclosure, the lender must file a suit against the borrower and obtain a decree of sale from the court with jurisdiction in the county where the property is located. If the court finds the borrower in default, it will give a set period to pay the delinquent amount plus costs. If the borrower doesn't pay within that period of time, the court will then order the property be sold.

A notice of the sale must be posted in at least three public places in the county. One must be at the county courthouse. In addition, the lender should publish the notice in two weekly publications printed in the county. The first publication must be at least four weeks before the date of sale and the second at a later time before the sale. If the borrower occupies and possesses the property, he must be served the notice at least twenty days prior to the sale. The sale must be at public auction, between 9:00 a.m. and 4:00 p.m. The date must be stated clearly in the notice of sale. The highest bid wins the auction.

Iowa borrowers can avoid a foreclosure suit by voluntarily conveying all of their rights in the property secured by the mortgage to the lender. If the lender accepts the conveyance from the borrower, the lender is given immediate access to the property. The lender must waive any rights to file for a deficiency judgment against the borrower if the property is voluntarily conveyed. In addition the borrower must sign a disclosure of notice and cancellation to indicate he is voluntarily giving up his rights to reclaim or occupy the property. The borrower and lender must file a joint document with the county recorder's office indicating they have chosen to proceed with the foreclosure using the voluntary foreclosure procedures.

If the borrower chooses to file for bankruptcy to stop a foreclosure, Iowa offers a homestead exemption at an unlimited property value provided the property does not exceed .5 acre in a town or city or 40 acres elsewhere.

Question 196. What are the foreclosure and homestead exemption rules specific to Kansas?

Kansas lenders can foreclose on a mortgage in default using the judicial foreclosure process. Usually, after the court orders a foreclosure, the property is auctioned to the highest bidder.

If a property is to be sold at a foreclosure auction, the notice of the time of sale must be advertised once a week for three consecutive weeks with the last publication being no more than fourteen days and no less than seven days before the sale. The borrower must receive a notice of the sale within five days of the first advertisement.

Unless the court specifies otherwise, the sale is held at the courthouse of the county in which the property is located. The highest bidder wins the sale and will receive a certificate of purchase. After the sale is confirmed, the winning bidder gets a sheriff's deed. The borrower has a right of redemption for twelve months from the date of the foreclosure sale. Lenders may sue for a deficiency judgment.

If the borrower decides to file for bankruptcy to stop a foreclosure, Kansas offers a homestead exemption of unlimited value as long as the property is less than 1 acre in a town or city or 160 acres on a farm.

Question 197. **What are the foreclosure and homestead exemption rules specific to Kentucky?**

Kentucky lenders can foreclose on a mortgage in default by using the judicial foreclosure process. Usually, the court decrees the amount of the borrower's debt and gives him a short time to pay. If the borrower doesn't pay within that time, the clerk of the court advertises the property for sale.

Property must be appraised prior to the scheduled date of foreclosure. If the foreclosure sale price is less than two-thirds of the appraised value, the borrower has one year from the date of the sale to redeem the property. To do so, he must pay the amount for which the property was sold plus interest.

Lenders can obtain a deficiency judgment against the borrower for the difference between the amount the borrower owed on the original loan and the foreclosure sale price, but only if the borrower was personally served with the lawsuit or failed to answer.

If the borrower chooses to file a bankruptcy to stop a foreclosure, Kentucky allows a homestead exemption of $5,000.

Question 198. **What are the foreclosure and homestead exemption rules specific to Louisiana?**

Louisiana lenders may foreclose on a mortgage in default by using one of two judicial foreclosure processes: executory and ordinary. The ordinary process involves filing a suit and getting a court order after which the property is sold.

The executory process takes place when the lender uses a mortgage that includes an "authentic act that imparts a confession of judgment," a statute unique to Louisiana meaning that the borrower signed and acknowledged the obligations of the mortgage in the presence of a notary public and two witnesses. This type of mortgage makes the foreclosure process easier for the lender because once the suit is filed and the original note and a certified copy of the mortgage is provided, the court will issue an order for the process to begin.

Once an executory process is ordered by the court, the borrower must then be served with a demand for the delinquent payments. The borrower has three days to pay or the court will order a writ of seizure. The sale of the property will be held after being advertised for thirty days.

Lenders may also sue to obtain a deficiency judgment. Buyers have no rights of redemption.

If the borrower chooses to file a bankruptcy to stop a foreclosure, Louisiana provides a $25,000 homestead exemption. If the debt is the result of catastrophic or terminal illness or injury one year before filing a bankruptcy, the value of the homestead exemption is unlimited provided the property is less than 5 acres in a city or town or 200 acres elsewhere in the state.

Question 199. **What are the foreclosure and homestead exemption rules specific to Maine?**

Maine lenders may foreclose on mortgages in default using either a judicial or strict foreclosure process. Although Maine does allow lenders to pursue foreclosure by judicial methods, which involves filing a lawsuit to obtain a court order to foreclose, it is only used in special circumstances. The primary method of foreclosure in Maine is strict foreclosure.

The strict foreclosure process is based on Maine's foreclosure doctrine, which states that the lender owns the property until the mortgage is paid in full. If the borrower breaks any conditions of the mortgage before being paid in full, the borrower loses any right to the property. The lender can take possession of the property or arrange for its sale.

The borrower has a redemption period of three months (for pre-1975 mortgages) or twelve months (post-1975 mortgages). If the lender takes possession of the property, it must hold possession of it for the entire redemption period to finalize the foreclosure. If the lender chooses to sell the property without taking possession of it first, it must file an initial suit and then wait until the end of the redemption period to sell the property according to special procedures set by the court. Lenders may file for a deficiency judgment, but it is limited to the difference between the fair market value, as determined by an appraisal, and the balance of the loan in default.

If the borrower chooses to file for bankruptcy to stop a foreclosure, Maine provides a homestead exemption up to $35,000. If the debtor has minor dependents or is over the age of sixty or is physically or mentally disabled, then the homestead exemption is $70,000.

Question 200. **What are the foreclosure and homestead exemption rules specific to Maryland?**

Maryland lenders that want to foreclose on a mortgage or deed of trust in default can use one of three methods: judicial foreclosure, an assent to decree, or nonjudicial foreclosure process. If the security instrument does not contain a power-of-sale clause or an assent-to-a-decree clause, the lender must file a suit against the borrower and obtain a decree of sale from a court that has jurisdiction in the county where the property is located before foreclosure proceedings can begin. The court determines whether a default has occurred.

If the court finds that a default has occurred, it sets the amount of the debt, interest, and costs then due and provides a reasonable time within which payment must be made if the borrower wants to keep the property. The court may order that if payment is not made within the time fixed in the order, the property must be sold to satisfy the debt.

If an assent-to-a-decree foreclosure exists in the mortgage or deed of trust, the lender must file a complaint to foreclose. It is easier than an ordinary foreclosure because a hearing does not need to be held prior to the foreclosure sale.

If a power-of-sale clause exists in the mortgage or deed of trust, a nonjudicial foreclosure process can be used. Lenders must still file with the court before the foreclosure process can begin, but a hearing is not necessary. Once foreclosure begins, the process includes the following:

- A notice of sale is published in a newspaper published in the county where the property is located at least once a week for three successive weeks. The first publication cannot be less than fifteen days prior to sale. The last publication cannot be more than one week prior to sale. The notice of sale must also be sent to the borrower at his last known address by certified and registered mail not more than thirty days and not less than ten days before the sale.
- The sale must be conducted by a person authorized to make the sale, such as the trustee or sheriff, and may take place immediately outside the courthouse entrance, on the property itself, or at the location advertised in the notice of sale.
- Within thirty days after the sale, the person authorized to make the sale must file a complete report of the sale with the court. The clerk of the court then issues a notice with a brief description identifying the property and stating the sale will be ratified unless appealed within thirty days after

the date of the notice. A copy of the notice will be published at least once a week in each of three successive weeks before the expiration of the thirty-day period in one or more county newspapers.

Lenders have three years to file for a deficiency judgment, which is limited to the balance of the loan in default after the foreclosure sale proceeds have been applied.

Maryland has no homestead exemption. If the borrower holds title as tenancy by the entirety, the property will be exempt from bankruptcy if the debts involved are owed by only one spouse.

Question 201. What are the foreclosure and homestead exemption rules specific to Massachusetts?

Massachusetts lenders may foreclose on deeds of trusts or mortgages in default using either a foreclosure-by-possession or a nonjudicial foreclosure process. If a lender chooses to use the foreclosure-by-possession process after the borrower defaults on the mortgage, the lender can take possession of the property by obtaining a court order, entering the property peaceably, and getting consent of the buyer. After the lender maintains possession peaceably for three years, the borrower loses all rights of redemption.

If a power-of-sale clause exists in a mortgage or deed of trust, a nonjudicial foreclosure process can be used. This process includes the following steps:

- Recording a notice of sale in the county where the property is located. The notice also must be sent, by registered mail, to the borrower at his last known address at least fourteen days prior to the foreclosure sale. In addition, it must be published once a week for three weeks, with the first publication at least twenty-one days before the sale, in a county newspaper of general circulation in the county where the property is located. The notice must include the place, time, and date of the foreclosure hearing, the date the mortgage was recorded, the borrower's name, the amount of the default, and the terms of the sale.

■ The sale must be by public auction on the date, time, and place specified in the notice of sale, and the property is sold to the highest bidder.

If the borrower wants to file for bankruptcy to stop the foreclosure of the property, Massachusetts offers a $500,000 bankruptcy exemption.

Question 202. **What are the foreclosure and homestead exemption rules specific to Michigan?**

Michigan lenders may foreclose on deeds of trusts or mortgages in default using either a judicial or nonjudicial foreclosure process. In judicial foreclosure, a court decrees the amount of the borrower's debt and gives him a short time to pay. If the borrower fails to pay within that time, the court issues a notice of sale.

If a power-of-sale clause exists in the deed of trust, a nonjudicial foreclosure can be used. Here is the nonjudicial foreclosure process:

■ A notice of sale must be published once a week for four weeks in a newspaper with general circulation in the county where the property is located. The notice must also be posted on the property at least fifteen days after the first notice of sale is published. The notice must contain the borrower's and lender's names, a description of the property, the terms of the sale, and the time, place, and date of the sale.

■ The trustee or the sheriff of the county may conduct the sale between the hours of 9:00 a.m. and 4:00 p.m. on the date specified in the notice of sale.

■ The sale must be made at public auction and sold to the highest bidder.

If the borrower wants to file for bankruptcy to stop the fore-closure of the property, a homestead exemption of $3,500 is given provided the property is on one lot in a town, village, or city or forty acres elsewhere. A spouse or child of a deceased owner may claim the homestead exemption. If the property is held as tenancy by the entirety, it may be exempt from debts owed by just one spouse.

Question 203. **What are the foreclosure and homestead exemption rules specific to Minnesota?**

Minnesota lenders may foreclose on deeds of trusts or mortgages in default using either a judicial or nonjudicial foreclosure process. The judicial process involves filing a lawsuit to obtain a court order to foreclose and must be used when no power-of-sale clause is present in the mortgage or deed of trust. Usually, after the court declares a foreclosure, the home is auctioned to the highest bidder. If there is a power-of-sale clause in the mortgage or deed of trust, a nonjudicial foreclosure is used. The process for a nonjudicial foreclosure includes the following steps:

- A notice of sale must contain the borrower's and lender's names, the original loan amount and current amount of default, the date of the mortgage, a description of the property, and the time, place, and date of the foreclosure sale and must be recorded in the county where the property is located.
- The sheriff of the county in which the property is located conducts the sale on the date specified in the notice of sale. The property is sold to the highest bidder, who will receive a certificate of sale.

Lenders may pursue a deficiency judgment, but it is limited to the difference between the fair market value of the property and the unpaid balance of the original loan. Borrowers have up to one year to redeem the property by paying the past-due amount on the loan. If the borrower wants to file for bankruptcy to stop a fore-closure, Minnesota offers a homestead exemption of $200,000. If the homestead is used for agricultural purposes, an exemption of $500,000 is provided. The property cannot exceed .5 acre in the city or 160 acres elsewhere.

Question 204. What are the foreclosure and homestead exemption rules specific to Mississippi?

Mississippi lenders may foreclose on deeds of trusts or mortgages in default using either a judicial or nonjudicial foreclosure process. The judicial process is used when no power-of-sale clause is present in the mortgage or deed of trust. Usually, after the court declares a foreclosure, the home is auctioned to the highest bidder.

If a power-of-sale clause exists in a mortgage or deed of trust, a nonjudicial foreclosure is used. The nonjudicial foreclosure process includes the following steps:

- The trustee records a notice of sale that includes the borrower's name and the date, time, and place of the sale in the county where the property is located. This notice must be posted at the courthouse door in the county where the property is located and published in a newspaper of general circulation in the county for a period of three consecutive weeks before the sale.
- The borrower may cure the default and stop the foreclosure before the foreclosure sale by paying the delinquent payments plus costs and fees.
- The sale may be held in the county where the property is located or in the county where the borrower resides. In either case, the sale must be conducted at the normal location for sheriff's sales within the given county. Borrowers who lose their property as the result of a nonjudicial foreclosure have no rights of redemption in Mississippi.
- The property is sold at public auction for cash to the highest bidder.

If the borrower chooses to file for bankruptcy to stop the foreclosure process, Mississippi provides a homestead exemption of $75,000. The property cannot exceed 160 acres.

Question 205. **What are the foreclosure and homestead exemption rules specific to Missouri?**

Missouri lenders may foreclose on a deed of trust or mortgages in default using either a judicial or nonjudicial foreclosure process. The judicial foreclosure process is used when no power-of-sale clause is present in the mortgage or deed of trust. Usually, after the court declares a foreclosure, the home is auctioned to the highest bidder.

If a power-of-sale clause is present in the mortgage or deed of trust, a nonjudicial foreclosure process can be used. Here is the way that process works:

- A notice of sale must be mailed to the borrower at his last known address at least twenty days prior to the scheduled day of sale. The notice of sale must also be published in a newspaper within the county.
- The sale is conducted by the trustee at public auction and sold to the highest bidder for cash. The lender may bid on the property. If the lender is the winning bidder, the borrower has twelve months to redeem the property.

If the borrower chooses to file for bankruptcy to stop the foreclosure, Missouri provides a homestead exemption of up to $15,000. Property held as tenancy by the entirety may be exempt against debts if they are owed by only one spouse.

Question 206. **What are the foreclosure and homestead exemption rules specific to Montana?**

Montana lenders may foreclose on deeds of trusts or mortgages in default using either a judicial or nonjudicial foreclosure process.

When a judicial foreclosure is used, the court decrees the amount of the borrower's debt and gives him a short time to pay. If the borrower does not pay the debt within the time given, the court issues a notice of sale. If a power-of-sale clause exists in a mortgage or deed of trust, the nonjudicial foreclosure process is used. This process includes the following steps:

- A notice of sale must be recorded in the county where the property is located. The notice is then sent, by registered or certified mail, to the borrower at his last known address at least 120 days before the foreclosure sale. In addition, it is published once a week for three successive weeks in a newspaper of general circulation in the county where the property is located and posted on the property at least twenty days before the foreclosure sale. The notice must include the time, date, and place of sale; the borrower's, lender's, and trustee's name; a description of both the property and the amount in default; and the book and page in the appropriate county clerk's office where the deed is recorded.
- The trustee must conduct the foreclosure sale between the hours of 9:00 a.m. and 4:00 p.m. at the courthouse in the county where the property is located. The property must be sold at public auction to the highest bidder.

Lenders may not obtain a deficiency judgment against the borrower, and the borrower has no rights of redemption. If the borrower chooses to file for bankruptcy to stop the foreclosure, Montana allows a $100,000 homestead exemption.

Question 207. **What are the foreclosure and homestead exemption rules specific to Nebraska?**

Nebraska lenders may foreclose on a mortgage in default using the judicial foreclosure process. The court decrees the amount of the borrower's debt and then gives him a short time to pay. If the borrower fails to pay within that time, the clerk of the court adver-tises the property for sale. The court may order the entire property to be sold or just a part of it. The sale can be delayed for up to nine months after the court's decree if the borrower files a written request for a delay with the clerk of the court within twenty days after the judge's order. If the borrower doesn't ask for the delay, the process of the sale of the property can start twenty days after the judgment. The borrower has the right to cure the default at any time while the suit is pending by paying the delinquent amount owed plus any interest and costs that have accrued.

The sheriff must give public notice of the time and place of the sale by posting the notice on the courthouse door, posting the notice in at least five other public places in the county where the property is located, and advertising the property for sale once a week for a period of four weeks in a newspaper published in the county. The court must confirm the sale after it takes place. Once the sale is confirmed, the borrower has no right of redemption.

If the borrower decides to file for bankruptcy to stop the foreclosure process, Nebraska allows up to $12,500 as a homestead exemption, but the property cannot exceed two lots in a village or city or 160 acres elsewhere.

Question 208. **What are the foreclosure and homestead exemption rules specific to Nevada?**

Nevada lenders may foreclose on deeds of trusts or mortgages in default using either a judicial or nonjudicial foreclosure process. The judicial process of foreclosure is used when no power-of-sale clause exists in the mortgage or deed of trust. Usually, after the court declares a foreclosure, the home is auctioned to the highest bidder. The borrower can redeem the property for up to twelve months after the sale if the judicial foreclosure process is used.

If a power-of-sale clause exists in the mortgage or deed of trust, a nonjudicial foreclosure is used. The process for this type of foreclosure is as follows:

- A notice of default and election to sell must be sent by certified mail, return receipt requested, to the borrower at his last known address on the date the notice is recorded in the county where the property is located. Beginning on the day after the notice of default and election are recorded with the county and mailed to the borrower, the borrower has between fifteen to thirty-five days to cure the default by paying the delinquent amount on the loan. The actual amount of time allowed depends on the date of the original deed of trust.

- An owner can stop the foreclosure process by filing an intent to cure with the public trustee's office at least fifteen days prior to the foreclosure sale. He must then pay the money needed to bring the loan current by noon the day before the foreclosure sale is scheduled.

- The foreclosure sale will be held at the place, time, and date stated in the notice of default and election.

Lenders have three months after the sale to try and obtain a deficiency judgment. Borrowers have no rights of redemption.

If the borrower decides to file for bankruptcy to stop the foreclosure, Nevada allows up to $200,000 as a homestead exemption.

Question 209. **What are the foreclosure and homestead exemption rules specific to New Hampshire?**

New Hampshire has five methods of foreclosure that can be used, including a judicial or nonjudicial foreclosure. One of three special methods may also be used: entry under process, entry and publication, or possession and publication.

The judicial foreclosure process is a strict foreclosure process where the lender files a complaint against the borrower and obtains a decree of sale from a court that has jurisdiction in the county where the property is located in order to start the foreclosure process. Usually, if the court finds the borrower in default, it will give the borrower a set period of time to pay the delinquent amount plus costs. If the borrower does not pay within that period of time, the court will order the property be sold. Anyone can bid at the foreclosure sale, including the lender.

If the mortgage or deed of trust has a power-of-sale clause, a nonjudicial foreclosure will be used. Here is how that type of foreclosure works:

- The lender records a notice of sale in the county where the property is located and mails the notice to the borrower at least twenty-five days before the sale. In addition, the lender publishes the notice once a week for three weeks, with the first publication appearing more than twenty days before the sale, in a newspaper with general circulation in the county where the property is located.
- The notice must include the time, date, and place of sale, a description of the property and the default, as well as a warning to the borrower. The warning must inform him that the property is going to be sold and explain any rights he may have to stop the foreclosure.
- The foreclosure sale must be held on the property itself unless the power-of-sale clause specifies a different location.

In addition to the traditional judicial and nonjudicial methods of foreclosure, New Hampshire also allows these special methods:

- Entry under process: With this method, the lender enters the property under process of law and maintains actual possession of the property for one year to complete the foreclosure.
- Entry and publication: With this method, the lender enters the property peaceably and takes continued, actual, peaceable possession for a period of one year. In addition, the lender publishes a notice stating the time of possession, the lender's and borrower's names, the date of the mortgage, and a description of the property in a newspaper of general

circulation in the county where the property is located. The notice must be published for three successive weeks, with the first publication appearing at least six months before the borrower's right to redeem has expired.

■ Possession and publication: With this method, the lender takes possession of the property and then publishes a notice stating that from and after a certain day, the property will be held for default of the mortgage and the borrower's rights to the property will be foreclosed. This notice must be published in a newspaper printed in the county where the property is located for three successive weeks and must give the borrower's and lender's names, the date of the mortgage, a description of the property, and the lender's intention to hold possession of the property for at least one year.

Borrowers have no rights of redemption when any of these three special methods of foreclosure is used.

If the borrower decides to file for bankruptcy to stop one of these foreclosure processes, New Hampshire allows a homestead exemption up to $100,000.

Question 210. **What are the foreclosure and homestead exemption rules specific to New Jersey?**

New Jersey lenders may foreclose on a mortgage in default by using the judicial foreclosure process. After the court decrees the amount of the borrower's debt, it gives the borrower a short time to pay. If the borrower fails to pay the debt within that time, the clerk of the court advertises the property for sale. Once the foreclosure process begins, a foreclosure notice must be posted in the county office where the property is located, posted on the property in foreclosure, and published in two newspapers in the county. The lender must also notify the borrower at least ten days prior to the foreclosure sale.

Lenders can obtain a deficiency judgment. Borrowers have a right to redemption and/or objection within ten days after the sale.

New Jersey offers no homestead exemption, but if the title of the property is held as tenancy by the entirety and the debt is owed by only one spouse, bankruptcy by the spouse in debt could stop the foreclosure because the spouse not in debt does have an exemption.

Question 211. What are the foreclosure and homestead exemption rules specific to New Mexico?

New Mexico lenders may foreclose on a mortgage in default by using the judicial foreclosure process. A court will decree the amount of the borrower's debt and give him a short time to pay. If the borrower doesn't pay within that time, the court will issue a notice of sale. The notice of sale must contain a legal description of the property, as well as state the place, time, and date of the sale. The sale must be at least thirty days after the notice of sale is issued. The property is then sold to the highest bidder on the date specified in the notice.

In most cases, the borrower has up to nine months to redeem the property by paying the amount of the highest bid at the fore-closure sale plus costs and interest. A nonjudicial foreclosure is only available for commercial and business properties valued at over $500,000.

If the borrower does decide to file for bankruptcy to stop the foreclosure, New Mexico offers a homestead exemption of up to $30,000.

Question 212. What are the foreclosure and homestead exemption rules specific to New York?

New York lenders may foreclose on deeds of trusts or mortgages in default using either a judicial or nonjudicial foreclosure process.

Using the judicial foreclosure process, the lender files a complaint against the borrower and obtains a decree of sale from a court having jurisdiction in the county where the property is located. Once that decree is issued by the court, foreclosure proceedings can begin. Usually, the court will give the borrower a set period of time to pay the delinquent amount plus costs. If the borrower doesn't pay within the time allotted, the court will order the property sold by the sheriff of the county or a referee. In most situations, the foreclosure sale is advertised for four to six weeks. The property is then sold by public auction to the highest bidder. Anyone may bid, including the lender.

After the property is sold, the officer conducting the sale must execute a deed to the purchaser. The officer must also pay the debt owed using the proceeds of the sale and then obtain a receipt for payment from the lender. Within thirty days after completing the sale, the officer must file a report of sale, which must include the receipt from the lender, with the clerk of the court. Unless otherwise ordered by the court, the sale cannot be confirmed until three months after the filing of the report of sale.

If the mortgage or deed of trust includes a power-of-sale clause, a nonjudicial foreclosure is used. Even though this type of foreclosure is allowed in New York, it is rarely used by lenders.

If the borrower decides to file for bankruptcy to stop the foreclosure, New York allows a $10,000 homestead exemption.

Question 213. What are the foreclosure and homestead exemption rules specific to North Carolina?

North Carolina lenders may foreclose on deeds of trusts or mortgages in default using either a judicial or nonjudicial foreclosure process. The judicial process involves filing a lawsuit to obtain a court order to foreclose. Usually, after the court declares a foreclosure, the home is auctioned to the highest bidder.

If the mortgage or deed of trust includes a power-of-sale clause, a nonjudicial foreclosure will be used. In North Carolina, a preliminary hearing must be held before a power-of-sale foreclosure can take place. Here is the process for a nonjudicial foreclosure:

- The lender must send a notice of sale by first-class mail to the borrower at least twenty days before the sale. He also must publish the notice in a newspaper of general circulation in the county where the property is located once a week for two successive weeks, with the last ad being published not less than ten days before the sale. In addition, the notice must be posted on the courthouse door for twenty days prior to the foreclosure sale. The notice must include the names of borrowers and lenders, as well as provide a description of the property. It also must state the date, time, and place of sale.
- The sale must be conducted at the courthouse in the county where the property is located between the hours of 10:00 a.m. and 4:00 p.m. The property is sold to the highest bidder.

Lenders may seek a deficiency judgment. Borrowers retain the right to redemption for ten days after the sale.

If the borrower decides to file for bankruptcy to stop the foreclosure, North Carolina allows a $10,000 homestead exemption. If the borrowers hold the property as tenancy by the entirety and only one spouse owes the debt, the property may be exempt from foreclosure.

Question 214. **What are the foreclosure and homestead exemption rules specific to North Dakota?**

North Dakota lenders may foreclose on a mortgage in default by using the judicial foreclosure process. A court decrees the amount of the borrower's debt and gives him a short time to pay. If the borrower doesn't pay within that time, the clerk of the court then advertises the property for sale.

In addition, North Dakota requires the lender to give the borrower no less than thirty days advance notice of its intent to foreclose. This notice must be sent by registered or certified mail no later than ninety days before the suit is filed and must contain a description of the property, the date and amount of the mortgage, the individual amounts due for principal, interest, and taxes due, and a statement that a lawsuit will be filed to foreclose on the property if the amount is not paid within thirty days of the date the notice was mailed. The borrower can stop the foreclosure by paying the delinquent amount plus foreclosure costs before the sale is confirmed by the court.

All sales in North Dakota must be made by the sheriff or his deputy in the county where the property is located. The property will be sold to the highest bidder, who will be issued a certificate of sale until the borrower's redemption period has ended. Borrowers typically have one year to redeem the property by paying the balance due on the loan plus costs. The time for redemption may be only six months if the mortgage includes short-term redemption rights. Lenders may be able to obtain a deficiency judgment against the borrower in North Dakota.

If the borrower decides to file for bankruptcy to stop a foreclosure, North Dakota allows up to an $80,000 homestead exemption.

Question 215. **What are the foreclosure and homestead exemption rules specific to Ohio?**

Ohio lenders may foreclose on a mortgage in default by using the judicial foreclosure process. A court decrees the amount of the borrower's debt and gives him a short time to pay. If the borrower doesn't pay in time, the clerk of the court then advertises the property for sale.

An appraisal of the property must be made by three disinterested freeholders of the county before the foreclosure sale. A copy of the appraised value must be filed with the court clerk, and the property must be offered for sale at a price of not less than two-thirds of the appraised value.

The notice of sale must be published once a week for three consecutive weeks in a newspaper of general circulation in the county in which the property is located before the foreclosure sale can take place. The sheriff will conduct the sale at the courthouse. The property is sold to the highest bidder.

Lenders can obtain a deficiency judgment. The borrower may redeem the property at any time before the court confirms the foreclosure sale by paying the amount of the judgment plus costs and interest.

If the borrower decides to file for bankruptcy to stop the foreclosure, Ohio allows a $5,000 homestead exemption. If the property is held as tenancy by the entirety, then the property may be exempt against debts if only one spouse owes the money.

Question 216. **What are the foreclosure and homestead exemption rules specific to Oklahoma?**

Oklahoma lenders may foreclose on deeds of trusts or mortgages in default using either a judicial or nonjudicial foreclosure process. Using a judicial process, lenders must file a lawsuit to obtain a court order to foreclose. After the court declares a foreclosure, the home is auctioned to the highest bidder.

Unless the borrower waives the right to an appraisal, the property must be appraised before the foreclosure sale, where it must be sold for at least two-thirds of the appraised value. A lender can sue for a deficiency judgment within ninety days after the sale. Borrowers cannot redeem the property once the court confirms the foreclosure sale.

If a power-of-sale clause exists in the mortgage or deed of trust, a nonjudicial foreclosure process likely will be used. Here are the steps for the nonjudicial foreclosure process:

- The lender must send the borrower a written notice of intention to foreclose by power of sale by certified mail to the borrower's last known address. The notice must describe the defaults of the borrower and give the borrower thirty-five days from the date the notice is sent to cure the problem. If the borrower cures the default in the specified time, the foreclosure can be stopped. If there have been three defaults, the lender need not send another notice of intent to foreclose, and after the fourth default in twenty-four months, provided proper previous notice was sent, no further notice is required.

■ The lender must record the notice in the county where the property is located within ten days after the borrower's thirty-five-day notice period has expired. The notice also must be published in a newspaper in the county where the property is located once a day for four consecutive weeks, with the first publication not less than thirty days before the sale. The notice must state the names of the borrower and lender, describe the property (including the street address), and state the time and place of sale.

■ The property must be sold at public auction to the highest bidder at the time and date specified in the notice. If the highest bidder at the sale is anyone other than the borrower, the winning bidder must pay by cash or certified funds 10 percent of the bid amount. If the highest bidder is unable to do so, the lender may proceed with the sale and accept the next highest bid.

If the borrower chooses to file for bankruptcy to stop the foreclosure process, Oklahoma allows a homestead exemption of unlimited value as long as the property does not exceed 1 acre in a city, town, or village or 160 acres elsewhere.

Question 217. **What are the foreclosure and homestead exemption rules specific to Oregon?**

Oregon lenders may foreclose on deeds of trusts or mortgages in default using either a judicial or nonjudicial foreclosure process. If they use the judicial process, it involves filing a lawsuit to obtain a court order to foreclose. If the court declares a foreclosure, the home is auctioned to the highest bidder. Borrowers may redeem the property by paying the purchase price with interest, the foreclosure costs, and the purchaser's expenses in operating and maintaining the property within 180 days after the date of sale. If the borrower wants to redeem the property, he must file a notice with the sheriff between two and thirty days.

If a power-of-sale clause exists in the mortgage or deed of trust, a nonjudicial foreclosure likely will be used. Here are the steps of the nonjudicial foreclosure process:

- The lender records a notice of default in the county where the property is located. The borrower and/or occupant of the property must be served with a copy of the notice at least 120 days before the scheduled foreclosure sale date. The notice also must be published once a week for four successive weeks, with the last notice being published at least twenty days prior to the foreclosure sale. The notice must include a property description, recording information on the trust deed, a description of the default, the sum owed on the loan, the lender's election to sell, and the date, time, and place of sale.
- The borrower may cure the default at any time before the foreclosure by paying all past-due amounts plus costs.
- The sale must be at auction to the highest bidder for cash. Any person, except the trustee, may bid at the sale.

The lender cannot obtain a deficiency judgment when a nonjudicial foreclosure is used.

If the borrower chooses to file for bankruptcy to stop a foreclosure, Oregon allows a homestead exemption of up to $25,000 ($33,000 for joint owners). The property cannot exceed one block in a town or city or 160 acres elsewhere.

Question 218. **What are the foreclosure and homestead exemption rules specific to Pennsylvania?**

Pennsylvania lenders must use the judicial foreclosure process to foreclose on a mortgage in default. The process starts when the lender sends a notice of intent to foreclose to the borrower, which must be sent by first-class mail to the borrower's last known address. The notice cannot be sent until the borrower is at least sixty days behind in his mortgage payments. In the notice, the lender must make the borrower aware that his mortgage is in default and that the lender intends to accelerate the mortgage payments if the borrower does not cure the default within thirty days, which means that the remaining balance of the original mortgage will come due immediately.

If the borrower does not cure the default by paying the past-due amount plus any late charges that have accrued within thirty days, the lender can file suit to obtain a court order to foreclose on the property. If the court finds in favor of the lender, it will issue an order of sale. The property is then sold at a sheriff's sale under the guidelines established by the court. The borrower can cure the default and prevent the sale at any time up to one hour before the sheriff's foreclosure sale.

Lenders have up to six months after the foreclosure sale to file for a deficiency judgment. Borrowers have no rights of redemption once the foreclosure sale is complete.

Pennsylvania does not allow a homestead exemption if the borrower files for bankruptcy to stop the foreclosure, but if the property is held as tenancy by the entirety, it may be exempt against debt owed by only one spouse.

Question 219. **What are the foreclosure and homestead exemption rules specific to Rhode Island?**

Rhode Island lenders may foreclose on mortgages or deeds of trusts in default in five different ways: judicial foreclosure, eviction, taking possession of the house, borrower voluntarily giving up possession, or nonjudicial foreclosure.

When a judicial foreclosure is used, the lender files a lawsuit to obtain a court order to foreclose. If the court declares a foreclosure, the home is auctioned to the highest bidder.

If a power-of-sale clause exists in the mortgage or deed of trust, a nonjudicial foreclosure process can be used. The steps include the following:

- The lender must mail a written notice to the borrower at his last known residence notifying him of the time and place of the sale by certified mail, return receipt requested, at least twenty days prior to the first publication of the sale.
- The lender must publish the sale notice in some public newspaper at least once a week for three successive weeks before the sale, with the first publication being at least twenty-one days before the day of sale.
- The notice must include the names of the borrower and lender, the mortgage date, the amount due, a description of the premises, and the time and place of sale. Any person may bid at the sale, including the lender.

In addition to these two common methods of foreclosure, two special methods are allowed in Rhode Island. One method allows the lender to take possession of the house as long as he does so peaceably and in the presence of two witnesses. Witnesses must give a certificate of possession, which must then be notarized. A second method allows borrowers to voluntarily give up possession of the property in the presence of a notary.

If the borrower decides to file for bankruptcy to stop foreclosure, Rhode Island allows up to a $200,000 homestead exemption.

Question 220. **What are the foreclosure and homestead exemption rules specific to South Carolina?**

South Carolina lenders must use the judicial foreclosure process to foreclose on a mortgage in default. The lender must file a complaint against the borrower and obtain a decree of sale from a court having jurisdiction in the county where the property is located before foreclosure proceedings can begin. If the court finds the borrower in default, it will give the borrower a set period of time to pay the delinquent amount plus costs. If the borrower fails to pay the amount within the set period of time, the court will order that the property be sold.

In most cases, this is the process for a foreclosure sale in South Carolina:

- A notice of sale that includes a description of the property, the time and place of sale, the borrower's name, and the lender's name is posted at the courthouse door and in two other public places at least three weeks prior to the date of sale. In addition, the notice must also be published in a newspaper of general circulation within the county where the property is located for the same three weeks.
- The sale is conducted by the sheriff at the county courthouse where the property is located. Foreclosure sales are held on the first Monday in each month between 11:00 a.m. and 5:00 p.m.
- The auction stays open for thirty days after the date of the public sale. During that time, anyone may place a bid higher than the last bid amount, and the successful purchaser is the one with the highest bid at the end of the thirty days.
- If there is no objection to the sale price of the property within three months of the date of sale, the sale is considered confirmed, and the sheriff makes any necessary deed endorsements.

Lenders in South Carolina may file for a deficiency judgment against the borrower. Borrowers have no rights of redemption. If the borrower decides to file for bankruptcy to stop the foreclosure process, South Carolina allows a $5,000 homestead exemption.

Question 221. **What are the foreclosure and homestead exemption rules specific to South Dakota?**

South Dakota lenders can foreclose on mortgages or deeds of trusts in default using either a judicial or nonjudicial foreclosure process. If a judicial process is used, the lender files a lawsuit to obtain a court order to foreclose. If the court declares a foreclosure, the home is auctioned to the highest bidder. If a power-of-sale clause exists in the mortgage or deed of trust, a nonjudicial foreclosure process is used. This process includes the following steps:

- The lender publishes a foreclosure notice once a week for four successive weeks in a newspaper of general circulation in the county where the property is located. In addition, at least twenty-one days before the sale, the lender must serve a written copy of the notice of foreclosure sale on the borrower and any interested lien holder. The notice must include the names of the borrower and lender, the mortgage date, the amount due, a description of the premises, and the time and place of sale.
- The sheriff of the county where the property is located conducts the sale. Any person including the lender may bid at the sale. The highest bidder wins the sale and will receive a certificate of sale.
- If the property is forty acres or less, and the mortgage contains a power-of-sale clause, then a 180-day period of redemption exists. If the property is abandoned, the time period is reduced to sixty days. Unless there are special short-term redemption provisions in the mortgage, borrowers may redeem within one year of the date of sale.

If the borrower decides to file for bankruptcy to stop the foreclosure, South Dakota allows an unlimited-value homestead exemption, provided the property does not exceed 1 acre in a town or 160 acres elsewhere.

Question 222. **What are the foreclosure and homestead exemption rules specific to Tennessee?**

Tennessee lenders can foreclose on deeds of trusts or mortgages in default using either a judicial or nonjudicial foreclosure process. If the judicial process is used, the lender must file a complaint against the borrower to obtain a decree of sale from a court that has jurisdiction in the county where the property is located in order to start foreclosure proceedings. If the court finds the borrower in default, it will give the borrower a set period of time to pay the delinquent amount plus costs. If the borrower doesn't pay on time, the court orders the property sold.

In most cases, in Tennessee, the mortgage or deed of trust includes a power-of-sale clause, and the nonjudicial foreclosure process is used. This process includes these steps:

- The lender publishes a notice of sale at least three different times in a newspaper published in the county where the property is located. The first publication must appear at least twenty days prior to the sale. If no newspaper is published in the county, the notice of sale must be posted at least thirty days in advance of the sale in at least five public places within the county. At least one of these notices must be placed at the courthouse door and another in the neighborhood of the property itself. In addition, the notice of sale must also be served upon the borrower at least twenty days before the date of sale if the borrower is in possession of the property.
- The sale must be held between the hours of 10:00 a.m. and 4:00 p.m. The sheriff of each county sets a minimum acceptable price for the property, which must be equal to

or greater than 50 percent of the fair market value. The property is sold for cash to the highest bidder.

- The successful bidder at the foreclosure sale will receive a certificate of sale and may be entitled to receive a deed once the borrower's right of redemption has expired. The borrower has a period of two years to redeem the property unless his right of redemption was waived in the original deed of trust.

Deficiency judgments are allowed in Tennessee.

If the borrower decides to file for bankruptcy to stop foreclosure, Tennessee allows a $5,000 homestead exemption ($7,500 for joint owners). Exemptions up to $25,000 are allowed if both spouses are over the age of sixty-two.

Question 223. **What are the foreclosure and homestead exemption rules specific to Texas?**

Texas lenders can foreclose on deeds of trusts or mortgages in default using either a judicial or nonjudicial foreclosure process. If a judicial foreclosure process is used, the lender files a lawsuit to obtain a court order to foreclose. If the court declares a foreclosure, the property is sold at auction to the highest bidder.

If a power-of-sale clause exists in a mortgage or deed of trust, a nonjudicial foreclosure sale is used. These are the steps required for a nonjudicial foreclosure:

- The lender starts the process by sending a letter of demand letting the buyer know he has twenty days to pay the delinquent payments or foreclosure proceedings will begin.
- Once the twenty-day period expires, and at least twenty-one days before the foreclosure sale, a foreclosure notice must be filed with the county clerk, mailed to the borrower at his last known address, and posted on the county courthouse door.

- The foreclosure sale must take place on the courthouse steps the first Tuesday of any month after the proper preliminary notices are completed. The winner is the highest bidder, who must pay by cash. Anyone may bid, including the lender, who bids by canceling out the balance (or some part of it) due on the note.

Lenders may obtain deficiency judgments, but they are limited to the difference between the fair market value of the property at the time of sale and the balance of the loan in default.

If the borrower decides to file for bankruptcy to stop foreclosure, Texas allows a homestead exemption of unlimited value provided the property doesn't exceed 10 acres in a town, village, or city or 100 acres elsewhere.

Question 224. What are the foreclosure and homestead exemption rules specific to Utah?

Utah lenders can foreclose on a mortgage in default by using the judicial or nonjudicial foreclosure process. If the judicial foreclosure process is used, the lender files a complaint against the borrower and obtains a decree of sale from a court that has jurisdiction in the county where the property is located to start foreclosure proceedings. If the court finds the borrower in default, it gives him a set period of time to pay the delinquent amount plus costs. If the borrower does not pay on time, the court orders the property sold. If the mortgage or deed of trust contains a power-of-sale clause, the nonjudicial foreclosure is used. These are the steps for a nonjudicial foreclosure:

- The lender publishes a notice of sale once a week for three consecutive weeks in a newspaper of general circulation in the county where the property is located. The last publication must be at least ten days but not more than thirty days before the sale. In addition, the notice of sale must also be posted at least twenty days before the date of sale is scheduled on the property to be sold and at the office of the county recorder in each county in which the property is located.

■ The place of sale must be included in the notice of sale, and the sale must be held between the hours of 8 a.m. and 5 p.m.

Borrowers do have a right of redemption in Utah. The court may extend the redemption time past the time allowed in regular judgments, so there is no set length of time. Lenders can obtain a deficiency judgment against the borrower for the difference between the amount the borrower owes on the original loan and the foreclosure sale price.

If the borrower decides to file for bankruptcy to stop the foreclosure, Utah allows a homestead exemption of $20,000.

Question 225. **What are the foreclosure and homestead exemption rules specific to Vermont?**

Vermont lenders can foreclose on a mortgage or deed of trust in default using either a judicial or nonjudicial foreclosure process. Vermont uses a strict foreclosure process in which the lender files a suit with the court when the borrower is in default to start the foreclosure process. The borrower will receive a summons to appear in court. If the court rules against the borrower, the lender can take possession of the property or schedule to sell it. For court foreclosures, the borrower usually is given six months from the time of the court ruling to redeem the property. The borrower must pay the full amount stipulated by the court to redeem.

If the property has a power-of-sale clause, the more common type of foreclosure is nonjudicial foreclosure. If a nonjudicial foreclosure is conducted, the lender mails a notice of the impending foreclosure to the borrower. This notice includes the amount in default that must be paid to stop the foreclosure and gives the borrower a deadline to cure the default of not less than thirty days.

The notice must be sent at least thirty days before a notice of sale is published.

A notice of sale can then be published that includes a description of the property, the lender's and borrower's names, mortgage date, and the time, day, location, and terms of the sale. The borrower must receive the notice of sale at least sixty days prior to the sale date. In addition, the notice is published once per week for three weeks in a local newspaper, with the first notice appearing no less than twenty-one days before the sale date. In nonjudicial foreclosures, the lender records the notice of sale in town records no less than sixty days before the sale instead of filing a foreclosure complaint in court. The borrower may stop the nonjudicial proceedings at any time prior to the sale by paying the default amount plus costs.

With either type of foreclosure process, the property is sold at public auction. Any person may bid. The property is sold to the highest bidder, and the borrower is entitled to receive any surplus from the sale proceeds. Within ninety days after a nonjudicial foreclosure sale, the property ownership is transferred free and clear to the winning bidder. Within ten days after a court foreclosure sale, the court either confirms the sale or orders a resale. If confirmed, the property ownership is transferred to the winning bidder.

If the borrower decides to file for bankruptcy to stop foreclosure, Vermont does not offer a homestead exemption. But if the borrowers hold the property as tenancy by the entirety, the property may be exempt if debts are owed by only one spouse.

Question 226. **What are the foreclosure and homestead exemption rules specific to Virginia?**

Virginia lenders may foreclose on deeds of trusts or mortgages in default using either a judicial or nonjudicial foreclosure process. To use the judicial foreclosure process, lenders file a lawsuit to obtain a court order to foreclose. If the court declares a foreclosure, the property will be auctioned to the highest bidder. The borrower has 240 days from the date of the sale to redeem the property by paying the amount for which the property was sold plus 6 percent interest.

If a power-of-sale clause exists in the mortgage or deed of trust, a nonjudicial foreclosure can be used. These are the steps for a nonjudicial foreclosure:

- Even if the deed of trust specifies how to advertise a fore-closure sale, Virginia statutes require ads to be published no less than once a day for three days. If the deed of trust does not provide for advertising, then the ad should be run once a week for four successive weeks. If the property is near a city, an ad on five different days, which may be consecutive, will be sufficient. The borrower must be mailed a copy of the advertisement or a notice with the same information at least fourteen days before the foreclosure sale. The ad must include anything required by the deed of trust and may include a legal description of the property, a street address, and a tax map identification or general information about the property's location. The notice must include the time, place, and terms of sale; the name of the trustee; and the address and phone number of a person who can answer inquiries about the foreclosure sale.
- Before the sale, the borrower may cure the default and stop the sale at any time by paying the lien debt, costs, and rea-sonable attorney's fees.
- The sale can't be held earlier than eight days after the first ad is published and no more than thirty days after the last advertisement is published. The property is sold at auction to the highest bidder. Any person other than the trustee can bid at the foreclosure sale, including a person who has submitted a written one-price bid. The property is sold to the highest bidder. The trustee can require bidders to place a cash deposit of up to 10 percent of the sale price, unless the deed of trust specifies a higher or lower amount.
- When the sale is complete, the proceeds first go to the expenses of executing the trust then to discharge all taxes,

levies, and assessments, with costs and interest if they have priority over the lien of the deed of trust. After that, liens are paid in order of their priority. Any remaining debts and obligations secured by the deed, and any liens of record inferior to the deed of trust, are then paid. All remaining proceeds go to the borrower. Lenders can obtain deficiency judgments without limits in Virginia.

If the borrower decides to file for bankruptcy to stop a foreclosure, Virginia allows a homestead exemption of up to $5,000.

Question 227. **What are the foreclosure and homestead exemption rules specific to Washington?**

Washington lenders can foreclose on deeds of trusts or mortgages in default using either a judicial or nonjudicial foreclosure process. If the judicial process is used, the lender files a lawsuit to obtain a court order to foreclose. If the court declares a foreclosure, the property is auctioned to the highest bidder. If a power-of-sale clause exists in a mortgage or deed of trust, a nonjudicial foreclosure can be used. The process for a nonjudicial foreclosure includes the following steps:

- The lender sends a notice of sale both by regular mail and by certified mail, return receipt requested, to the borrower at his last known address. In addition, the lender will send the notice by regular mail to the attorney of record for the borrower. Notices must be sent not less than thirty days prior to the day of sale. In addition, the sheriff must publish a notice of the sale once a week, consecutively, for four weeks, in any daily or weekly legal newspaper of general circulation in the county in which the property is located and post the notice in two public places, one of which must be the courthouse door in the county where the sale is to take place. These notices must be posted for at least four weeks prior to the day of sale. The notice must include the time and place of the foreclosure sale, the names of the parties to the deed, the date of the deed, recording information, a property description, the terms of the sale, and the borrower's rights (or lack of rights) to redemption.

- The borrower has up to eleven days before the sale to stop the foreclosure process by paying his past-due payments plus expenses, including trustee and attorney fees.
- The foreclosure sale must be done by auction between 9:00 a.m. and 4:00 p.m. at the courthouse door on Friday. The sale cannot be conducted less than ninety days from the date of default. The highest bidder gets a certificate of sale.

Unless redemption rights have been precluded, the borrower has eight months after the sale to redeem the property by paying the amount of the highest bid at the foreclosure plus interest.

If the nonjudicial process is used by the lender, he cannot sue for a deficiency judgment. On judicial foreclosure sales, the borrower can be sued for a deficiency, unless the property is abandoned for six months before the decree of foreclosure.

If the borrower decides to file for bankruptcy to stop the foreclosure, Washington allows a homestead exemption of up to $40,000.

Question 228. **What are the foreclosure and homestead exemption rules specific to Washington, D.C.?**

Washington, D.C., lenders use a nonjudicial process to foreclose on deeds of trusts in default. The terms of sale should be included in the deed of trust, but if they are not established in the deed of trust, the lender must obtain a court order that does specify the terms of the sale. Before a foreclosure sale can take place, the lender must send a written notice by certified mail, return receipt requested, to the borrower at his last known address. In addition, this notice must also be sent to the mayor of the District of Columbia or his designated agent.

Both notices must be sent at least thirty days prior to the sale, with the thirty-day period beginning on the day the notice is received by the mayor. This notice must be given in addition to any notices set forth by the court, the mortgage, or the deed of trust. Washington, D.C., lenders may obtain a deficiency judgment against the borrower for the difference between the foreclosure sale amount and the amount remaining on the original loan. The borrower has no rights of redemption.

If the borrower decides to file for bankruptcy to stop foreclosure, Washington, D.C., offers a homestead exemption for any property that is declared as a residence. If the property is held as tenancy by the entirety, it may be exempt from debts owed by only one spouse.

Question 229. **What are the foreclosure and homestead exemption rules specific to West Virginia?**

West Virginia lenders can foreclose on a deed of trust or mortgage in default using either a judicial or nonjudicial foreclosure process. If a judicial foreclosure is used, the lender files a lawsuit to obtain a court order to foreclose. If the court declares a foreclosure, the property is auctioned to the highest bidder.

If a power-of-sale clause exists in the mortgage or deed of trust, then a nonjudicial foreclosure can be used. The nonjudicial process includes the following steps:

- The lender posts a notice of sale on the front door of the courthouse for the county in which the property is located as well as three other public places, one of which must be the property itself, at least twenty days prior to the sale. In addition to the posted notices, a notice must be served upon the borrower and subordinate lien holders at least twenty days prior to the foreclosure sale. Plus, the notice must be published as a legal advertisement in the county where the property is located once a week for four weeks. The notice should include the time and place of the foreclosure sale, the names of the parties to the deed, the date of the deed, recording information, a property description, and the terms of the sale.

- The sale must be held at the time and place stated in the foreclosure notice. The sale will be completed by public auction to the highest bidder. Unless the deed specifies different terms of the sale, the buyer must pay one-third of the bid amount in cash at the sale.

Lenders are usually not permitted to sue for deficiency. Borrowers have no rights of redemption.

If the borrower decides to file for bankruptcy to stop the foreclosure, West Virginia allows a homestead exemption of up to $25,000.

Question 230. **What are the foreclosure and homestead exemption rules specific to Wisconsin?**

Wisconsin lenders can foreclose on a deed of trust or mortgage in default using either a judicial or nonjudicial foreclosure process. If the lender uses a judicial foreclosure, it must file a lawsuit to obtain a court order to foreclose. If the court declares a foreclosure, the property is auctioned to the highest bidder. No sale may be made for one year from the date the judgment is entered unless the lender waives the right to a deficiency. If the lender waives the right to a deficiency judgment, he only has to wait six months for the sale (two months if the property is abandoned). The borrower can consent to an earlier sale.

If a power-of-sale clause exists in a mortgage or deed of trust, a nonjudicial foreclosure can be used. These are the steps for a nonjudicial foreclosure:

- The lender must record his intent to foreclose with the county prior to the time the first notice of foreclosure is published. The notice, which must include the time and place of the sale, should be published once a week for six consecutive weeks in a newspaper that is published in the county where the property is located. In addition, the notice must be served upon the borrower in the same manner as he would be served in any civil lawsuit. If the borrower can't be found, the notice is posted in a conspicuous spot on the mortgaged property, and the occupant is served. The notice must specify the names of the borrower and lender, the date the mortgage was recorded, the amount due at the date of the notice, a property description, and the time and place of the sale.

- The sale must be held at the time and place stated in the foreclosure notice. The winning bidder receives a certificate of purchase.
- The borrower has twelve months to redeem the property by paying the amount of the highest bid at the foreclosure sale plus interest, unless the sale is confirmed by the court. Wisconsin law does allow for a foreclosure sale to be confirmed by court order. If the lender states his intentions in the application for sale confirmation, he may file a deficiency suit. Otherwise, deficiency suits are not permitted by Wisconsin law.

If the borrower decides to file for bankruptcy, Wisconsin allows a homestead exemption of up to $40,000.

Question 231. **What are the foreclosure and homestead exemption rules specific to Wyoming?**

Wyoming lenders can foreclose on a deed of trust or mortgage in default using either a judicial or nonjudicial foreclosure process. If the lender uses a judicial foreclosure, he must file a lawsuit to obtain a court order to foreclose. If the court declares a foreclosure, the property is auctioned to the highest bidder. If the mortgage or deed of trust includes a power-of-sale clause, the property can be sold using a nonjudicial foreclosure process. This process includes the following steps:

- The lender must serve the recorded owner and the person in possession of the property a written notice of intent to foreclose on the mortgage by advertisement and sale by certified mail, with return receipt, at least ten days before the first publication of a notice of sale.
- A notice of sale is then published at least once a week for four consecutive weeks in a newspaper printed in the county where the property is located. The notice must include the name of the borrower, the lender, the date of the mortgage and when it was recorded, the amount of the default, a description of the property, and the time and place of sale.
- The sale must be held at the front door of the courthouse of the county in which the property is located between the hours of 9:00 a.m. and 5:00 p.m. The sale is conducted by the person indicated in the mortgage or by the sheriff or deputy sheriff of the county. Anyone may bid, including the lender. The highest bidder receives a certificate of purchase.
- The borrower has three months from the date of sale to redeem the property by paying the amount of the purchase price or the amount bid by the mortgagee plus interest at the rate of 10 percent from the date of sale. He also must pay any assessments or taxes and the amount due on any prior lien paid by the purchaser after the purchase, with interest.

Lenders can obtain deficiency judgments in Wyoming.

If the borrower does decide to file for bankruptcy to stop a foreclosure, Wyoming does not offer a homestead exemption. If the property is held as tenancy by the entirety, the property may be exempt from debts owed by only one spouse.

Chapter **13**

FIXING UP AND FLIPPING YOUR FORECLOSURE PURCHASE

You can be almost certain you will need to do some repairs before you will be able to sell a foreclosure property that you buy. In most cases, a homeowner nearing foreclosure does not make any repairs or may even cause some damage as he faces the financial stress involved. This chapter focuses on how to fix up a property for sale and how to sell your purchase quickly.

Question 232. What are the key elements of a property fix-up plan?

When you plan your fix-up, remember you are fixing up the property for a fast sale. You want it in marketable condition, but it does not have to meet your standards for a dream home. Basically, what you need to do is give the property a thorough cleaning and a cosmetic facelift both inside and out. How the property looks from the curb is very important, so be sure to clean up the landscaping and put on a fresh coat of paint.

As soon as the property is closed, you must be ready to get to work, so plan your budget and get cost estimates the same day that you close (if you haven't done it already). If you aren't able to do the necessary work professionally, hire a contractor. You should monitor the work and be sure it is up to the quality you expect.

You should set a schedule your contractor agrees to and put the completion date in the contract. Make sure the term *time is of the essence* is in the contract, and specify penalties if the job is late. You may even want to offer a bonus if the job is completed early to get the work done quickly.

Question 233. **How do you find reputable repairmen and contractors?**

If you don't already know reputable repairmen and contractors, talk with friends and family who have had work done at their homes. Be sure that anyone you hire is a licensed and insured contractor, repairman, or tradesman. Don't take someone's word and handshake. Insist that the bid be done in writing, and specify exactly what will be done for the price quoted.

Question 234. **What is the importance of hiring licensed and insured contractors?**

You will find lots of scam artists who promise to do work but don't complete it or don't finish on time. You can avoid many problems by being sure that you hire only licensed and insured contractors. If the contractors are not insured and someone gets hurt in your house, you could get stuck with thousands in medical bills.

To be sure a contractor is licensed and insured, ask to see copies of his licenses, worker's compensation insurance certificate, general liability insurance certificate, and automobile license certificate.

Question 235. **Why are written estimates important for all fix-up projects?**

Written estimates are for your protection to make sure the work you want done is included in the estimate. The estimate should include a detailed description of the work to be done, with a work schedule for start and completion of the job. You should also be certain that any materials that are needed are specified in the work order.

If building permits are needed for the job, be sure that the work order indicates who will be responsible for getting the permits. In most cases, permits should be the responsibility of the licensed contractor.

In addition, the estimate should detail the costs of the job and the payment schedule. For example, if you are going to pay 50 percent up front for materials and 50 percent on completion, that should be stated in writing. The written estimate should also state any warranties covering workmanship and materials.

Question 236. **What is a construction lien law, and how can it impact your fix-up project?**

Any time you have work done on your house and a contractor was not paid in full, he can file a mechanic's lien against your property. You want to be sure that everyone who works on the property signs a waiver and release of lien upon final payment. Read question 48, which discusses mechanic's liens, to understand what can happen if you don't get release of liens for each person who worked on the house.

Question 237. **What is the Worksite CD, and how can I get it free?**

Home Depot offers a great tool you can use to estimate and manage jobs, called the *Worksite CD*, which lists building materials and includes software to help you cost out a job. You can even create the estimate and send in the order automatically over the Internet to Home Depot.

Another useful feature is that the estimate can be exported to QuickBooks, if you use that accounting software, so you can generate invoices. You can pick up the *Worksite CD* at the contractor help desk of Home Depot.

Question 238. **Why is it important to fix up the exterior first?**

Always do the work on the exterior of the property first to make the property look more enticing to prospective buyers. You'll need to pressure-wash the walkways and driveways as well as the exterior services of the house itself. The pressure wash could expose additional work that needs to be done, especially if you find building materials that need to be replaced. Once all the dirt has been cleaned away, you can decide if a paint job is needed as well.

Once the house looks good from the outside, you can even post a for-sale sign and begin to generate interest unless there is a lot of work to do on the inside that may take a few weeks or months. If you get an interested caller before you are ready to show the house, you will only be able to delay them for a few days, so don't post a for-sale sign too far before you're actually ready to show the property.

Question 239. **How do you eliminate odors?**

Odors can turn off a potential buyer as soon as he walks in the door, so be sure to eliminate any odors before starting to show the property. One of the best odor eliminators, put out by Neutron Industries, is called NI-712 Orange Odor Eliminator. The product has even been proven to make skunk odors disappear quickly.

Odors that NI-712 eliminates include cigar and cigarette smoke, spoiled food, urine, vomit, and pet odors. You can call Neutron Industries at 888-712-7127 for more information and to get pricing.

Question 240. **How do you choose your colors?**

You should always choose neutral, light colors when painting the property. Ride around the neighborhood and get a sense for how houses are painted on the exterior, and pick a popular combination that fits well in the neighborhood.

Inside the home, it's best to paint using white or off white. That looks bright and clean and makes it easy for the buyer to paint if he wants to add other colors. Paint the walls using good quality flat latex, and use a semi-gloss enamel paint for the trim and doors.

Question 241. **Why should you use professionals for cleaning?**

It might cost you a bit more, but hire a professional to clean the property. The work will be done quickly, and the professional will know how to deal with any difficult spots. You may be able to find a good professional cleaner by talking with a small builder in the area. These firms usually hire an outside professional to do a final clean on the home after construction who knows how to deal with any paint spills or other things that may come up after the contractor completes the work.

Question 242. **Why should you always carefully inspect any work before making final payment?**

Before giving the contractor a final payment, be sure you have done a complete and thorough inspection. Once the contractor has his money, you won't find it easy to get him to come back to fix anything. Money due can be a powerful motivator to get someone to finish up the small items that still need to be done.

You may find problems after you've paid the contractor, and a good contractor will back his work. But once he packs up all his equipment and moves on to another job, it's very expensive for him in both time and money to come back to the job. Save yourself and the contractor the hassle and battles by doing a careful inspection while he's still at the home, waiting for final payment.

Question 243. **How do you calculate the resale value of your property after fix-up?**

Your first step is to figure out how much you spent finding, buying, and fixing up the property. Keep a running tally on each house from the time you start your research. As part of that research, you should have listings of comparable homes so you know what the market potential is for the house.

Price your house to sell by keeping as close as you can to the lowest prices for comparable homes. If you've done your job, the house should be in move-in condition and attractive to any buyer who walks in. If your house is in the best condition, you should be able to get a quick sale.

Question 244. **How do you market your fix-up properties using the Internet?**

Properties in the United States can be very attractive to international buyers, so don't hesitate to use the Internet to promote a property you have for sale. Getting people to view property you advertise on the Internet can be difficult if you try to set up your own page, so it's best to work with an established real estate Web site. One good one is ForSalebyOwner.com (*www.forsalebyowner. com*), which already generates heavy Web traffic because of its reputation. When you go to the Web site, click on the tab titled "Sell a Home," and you'll find a wealth of information about how to market your home on the Internet.

Question 245. What should you include in an e-mail to interested buyers?

Once you are contacted by buyers, be sure you have an effective e-mail ready to send back. This e-mail should include the property address, description of the property, sale price and terms, location of the property, and driving directions.

You can attach a couple of pictures, but be sure that you minimize their size so they don't create too large a file for those seeking information to download.

Question 246. What type of ads should you place in local newspapers?

Classified ads are the best, but pay a little extra for an ad that you can box and make it look a bit more professional. Always include your phone number, a link to the listing on the Internet, and an e-mail address. If you want to limit your calls, specify any terms that the potential buyer must meet to purchase the home, such as a minimum down payment or a top credit score.

Question 247. What type of signage should you put on the property?

Don't just buy a pre-printed for-sale sign and write in a contact number. That doesn't look very professional. You can have a sign made up that includes the "Home for Sale" and your contact information by phone and e-mail. You also can include a Web site for your properties if you have one on the Internet.

Question 248. **How should you work with real estate brokers?**

You can work with real estate brokers, but don't list the property with them. Let brokers know that you will pay a commission if they bring a buyer to you. Offer a commission that would be the same split the broker would get if he sold the listing of another broker.

A broker may require you to sign a contract specifying the split. You can do that, but be certain you don't sign any contract that gives the broker exclusive rights to sell the property.

Question 249. **How do you prequalify your potential buyers?**

You need to prequalify any interested potential buyers before spending time with them. Some key questions to ask are if they have money for a down payment and how much they have. You should ask what their current rent is and how much they can afford to pay each month on the house. Find out if they have a good credit rating or if there are problems with their credit. Ask how quickly they can close on the property.

If the answers you get don't meet the requirements you set in your mind, politely tell the person that he doesn't qualify for this house, but you'll keep him in mind if another possibility comes up in the future. Keep buyers' information if you think they may be a good prospect for another deal. Toss it if you don't think they could ever get a loan.

Question 250. **How can you use seller financing to get a quick sale to a qualified buyer?**

You can consider financing the home partially yourself to get a quick sale, but be sure you do your homework on the buyer. Require him to fill out a standard loan application that any financial institution would request.

Then you should get a copy of the buyer's consumer credit file. In addition, you should order a criminal background check. There are numerous Web sites on line that you can use to request a criminal background check. Evaluate the reports that you get, and determine whether or not you consider the buyer to be a good risk.

INDEX OF QUESTIONS

166 The 250 Questions Everyone Should Ask About Buying Foreclosures

Chapter 2:
Understanding Foreclosure Basics

18. What is foreclosure?

19. What is pre-foreclosure?

20. What are the four phases of foreclosure?

21. How do most lenders handle delinquent loans?

22. What are demand letters?

23. What is default status?

24. Can a loan be reinstated that is in default status?

25. What is a notice of default?

26. How does a notice of default work?

27. What information is included in a foreclosure notice?

28. Are foreclosure notices published in the newspaper?

29. What is a mortgage estoppel letter?

30. What must a lender do before foreclosing on or repossessing a home?

31. What is judicial foreclosure?

32. How does the judicial foreclosure process work?

33. What is nonjudicial foreclosure?

34. How does the nonjudicial foreclosure process work?

35. What is a power-of-sale foreclosure?

36. What is a no-power-of-sale foreclosure?

37. How do FHA and VA foreclosure rules differ from conventional loans?

38. How does the FHA counsel borrowers on the verge of defaulting?

39. What is special forbearance?

40. What is a due-on-sale or acceleration clause?

Chapter 3:
Looking at Liens

63. What are homeowners' association liens?

64. What are subordinate lien holders?

65. What is a junior lien holder?

66. What is a senior lien holder?

67. What is a lot-book report?

Chapter 4:
Buying a Property During the Lis Pendens Phase

68. What is lis pendens?

69. When does lis pendens begin?

70. What is posted as part of the lis pendens notice?

71. How do you find lis pendens properties?

72. How do you convince an owner to sell during the lis pendens phase?

73. How do you write a contract during the lis pendens phase?

74. How do you close on a deal during the lis pendens phase?

Chapter 5:
Buying a Pre-Foreclosure

75. What is a pre-foreclosure?

76. What are the benefits of buying a pre-foreclosure?

77. What are the steps in buying a pre-foreclosure?

78. How do you find property owners who are in default or facing foreclosure?

79. How do you contact property owners in default or facing foreclosure?

80. How do you verify loan information for loans in default?

Chapter 6:
Buying a Property Using a Short-Payoff Sale

101. What is a short-sale proposal letter?

102. What is a "borrower's authorization to release information"?

103. What is a borrower's short-sale application?

104. What is the borrower's financial statement?

105. What must the borrower supply regarding his financial history?

106. What are market comparables, and should you provide them?

107. How can you get the lender to pay repair costs?

108. How much cash do you need to finance a short-sale transaction?

109. Who is and is not eligible to buy a pre-foreclosure property as a short-payoff transaction?

110. Why are property owners reluctant to accept a short-sale?

111. What are the tax consequences of a short-sale?

112. How is the value of the property determined in a short-sale transaction?

113. What are the unique provisions of a short-payoff transaction if it is an FHA property?

114. What are the unique provisions of a short-sale if it is a VA property?

Chapter 7:
Buying a Property During a Foreclosure Sale

115. What is a public foreclosure auction?

116. How do you find properties to be auctioned?

117. What is an "as is" sale?

118. How do you research a property before auction?

119. How do you know what to bid?

120. How do you assess the condition of the property?

Chapter 8:
After a Foreclosure Sale

142. How do you find VA REOs?

143. What terms will the lender offer you on financing the property?

144. How much cash will you need?

145. What type of qualification process will you need to go through?

Chapter 9:
Bankruptcies and the Foreclosure Process

146. What is a bankruptcy?

147. Can an owner stop a foreclosure through bankruptcy?

148. What is a Chapter 7 bankruptcy?

149. What is a Chapter 11 bankruptcy?

150. What is a Chapter 13 bankruptcy?

151. What is a bankruptcy trustee?

152. What is an automatic stay?

153. How can owners use the stay process to avoid foreclosure?

Chapter 10:
Escrow and Closing

154. What is escrow?

155. How do you pick an escrow holder?

156. What are escrow instructions?

157. What is an escrow closing?

158. What is a quick-cash system?

159. What is a closing statement?

160. What is title insurance?

Chapter 12:
Discovering State-by-State Foreclosure and Homestead Exemption Rules

181. What are the foreclosure and homestead exemption rules specific to Alabama?

182. What are the foreclosure and homestead exemption rules specific to Alaska?

183. What are the foreclosure and homestead exemption rules specific to Arizona?

184. What are the foreclosure and homestead exemption rules specific to Arkansas?

185. What are the foreclosure and homestead exemption rules specific to California?

186. What are the foreclosure and homestead exemption rules specific to Colorado?

187. What are the foreclosure and homestead exemption rules specific to Connecticut?

188. What are the foreclosure and homestead exemption rules specific to Delaware?

189. What are the foreclosure and homestead exemption rules specific to Florida?

190. What are the foreclosure and homestead exemption rules specific to Georgia?

191. What are the foreclosure and homestead exemption rules specific to Hawaii?

192. What are the foreclosure and homestead exemption rules specific to Idaho?

193. What are the foreclosure and homestead exemption rules specific to Illinois?

208. What are the foreclosure and homestead exemption rules specific to Nevada?

209. What are the foreclosure and homestead exemption rules specific to New Hampshire?

210. What are the foreclosure and homestead exemption rules specific to New Jersey?

211. What are the foreclosure and homestead exemption rules specific to New Mexico?

212. What are the foreclosure and homestead exemption rules specific to New York?

213. What are the foreclosure and homestead exemption rules specific to North Carolina?

214. What are the foreclosure and homestead exemption rules specific to North Dakota?

215. What are the foreclosure and homestead exemption rules specific to Ohio?

216. What are the foreclosure and homestead exemption rules specific to Oklahoma?

217. What are the foreclosure and homestead exemption rules specific to Oregon?

218. What are the foreclosure and homestead exemption rules specific to Pennsylvania?

219. What are the foreclosure and homestead exemption rules specific to Rhode Island?

220. What are the foreclosure and homestead exemption rules specific to South Carolina?

221. What are the foreclosure and homestead exemption rules specific to South Dakota?

Chapter 13:
Fixing Up and Flipping Your Foreclosure Purchase

236. What is a construction lien law, and how can it impact your fix-up project?

237. What is the Worksite CD, and how can I get it free?

238. Why is it important to fix up the exterior first?

239. How do you eliminate odors?

240. How do you choose your colors?

241. Why should you use professionals for cleaning?

242. Why should you always carefully inspect any work before making final payment?

243. How do you calculate the resale value of your property after fix-up?

244. How do you market your fix-up properties using the Internet?

245. What should you include in an e-mail to interested buyers?

246. What type of ads should you place in local newspapers?

247. What type of signage should you put on the property?

248. How should you work with real estate brokers?

249. How do you prequalify your potential buyers?

250. How can you use seller financing to get a quick sale to a qualified buyer?

Index